yOung
Exceptional
children

Monograph Series No. 3

Teaching Strategies:
What to do to Support Young
Children's Development

**THE DIVISION FOR EARLY CHILDHOOD
OF THE COUNCIL FOR EXCEPTIONAL CHILDREN**

Michaelene Ostrosky and Susan Sandall
Co-Editors

Published and Distributed by:

SOPRIS
WEST
4093 Specialty Place • Longmont, CO 80504
(303) 651-2829 • FAX (303) 776-5934
www.sopriswest.com

1380 Lawrence St., Suite 650 • Denver, CO 80204
(303) 556-3328 • FAX (303) 556-3310
www.dec-sped.org

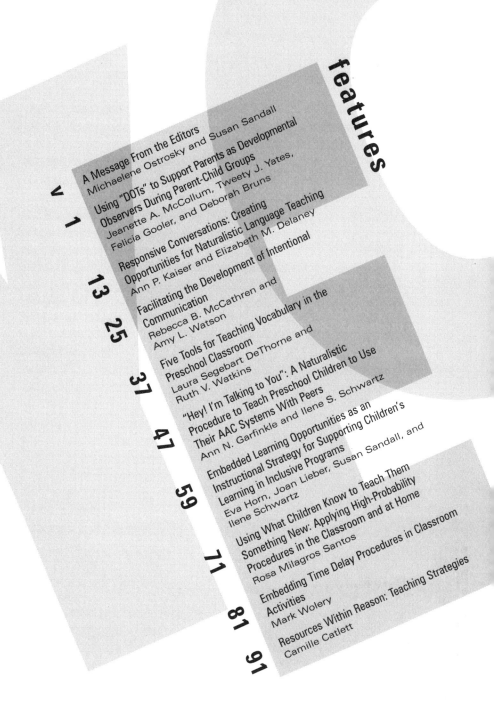

features

A Message From the Editors

Welcome to the third volume of the *Young Exceptional Children Monograph Series*. In this volume we focus on the topic of effective teaching strategies for young children with disabilities and other special needs. One of our goals within this monograph was to link the articles to *DEC Recommended Practices in Early Intervention/Early Childhood Special Education* (Sandall, McLean, & Smith, 2000). The articles in this monograph highlight practices found in Chapter 3, *Child-Focused Interventions*, as well as other practices related to direct services. In many cases the articles extend the practices by providing additional information and evidence and by providing tips and techniques that you can use in your classroom or other intervention setting.

Interestingly, the authors make some consistent points across the eight articles. They all write of the importance of planning. This entails careful selection of an appropriate teaching strategy (or strategies), developing instructional programs, and ensuring that teaching occurs. The authors also write about embedding or incorporating careful instruction within ongoing activities and routines. And, as some point out, this is more easily said than done.

The first article, by Jeanette McCollum and her colleagues, offers an approach for working with very young children and their parents. This approach is built on the power and importance of relationships. The focus is on helping parents become more sensitive and responsive observers of their own child's development and learning. The article will guide readers in the use of "developmental observation topics" within parent-child groups.

The importance of early communication is underscored by the inclusion of several articles. Kaiser and Delaney write about the importance of conversations between children and their teachers. This article gives teachers a set of responsive interaction strategies to engage children in conversation and then use the conversation to teach language behaviors. The approach described by McCathren and Watson is aimed at young children who may be struggling with the transition from preintentional to intentional communication. They describe strategies for teachers to use to help children make this very important transition. DeThorne and Watkins address five strategies that can be used by regular and special education teachers and staff to facilitate children's vocabulary development. Garfinkle and Schwartz focus on children who are using augmentative or adaptive communication (AAC) systems. In particular, the naturalistic strategies they describe will help children have meaningful communicative interactions with their peers.

The importance of thoughtful and careful planning is highlighted in the remaining three articles. Providing young children with special needs multiple opportunities to practice new skills is critical. Eva Horn and her colleagues define an instructional strategy they have termed embedded learning opportunities (ELO), and they describe a planning process for embedding learning opportunities across the preschool day. Next, Rosa Milagros Santos describes high-probability procedures. These are strategies that early childhood special education teachers can use to increase the complexity and duration of children's play, engagement, appropriate behavior, and learning. In her article she defines high-probability procedures, describes the components of this intervention strategy, and suggests some issues to consider when choosing to use high-probability procedures. Finally, Mark Wolery provides readers with a step-by-step description for planning and using a specialized and effective teaching procedure: time delay. Time delay has been demonstrated to be an effective teaching method for the acquisition and use of a variety of important skills, and he illustrates how the time delay procedure can be embedded and distributed within classroom activities.

We hope that the articles in this monograph accomplish a number of things. First, we hope that you see yourself in some of the articles and that you are validated for what you are already doing. Second, we hope that they shed new light on your practices or give you some new ideas. Third, we hope that they remind you that we, as a field, have evidence that we must use to guide our planning and teaching (Wolery, 2000). We thank the authors and the reviewers who contributed to this volume of the *Young Exceptional Children* Monograph Series.

References

Sandall, S., McLean, M. E., & Smith, B. J. (2000). *DEC recommended practices in early intervention/early childhood special education*. Longmont, CO: Sopris West.

Wolery, M. (2000). Recommended practices in child-focused interventions. In S. Sandall, M. E. McLean, & B. J. Smith (Eds.), *DEC recommended practices in early intervention/early childhood special education* (pp. 29-37). Longmont, CO: Sopris West.

Co-Editors: Michaelene Ostrosky   Susan Sandall
(217) 333-0260   (206) 543-4011
ostrosky@uiuc.edu   ssandall@u.washington.edu

Using "DOTs" to Support Parents as Developmental Observers During Parent-Child Groups

Jeanette A. McCollum, Ph.D., University of Illinois at Urbana-Champaign
Tweety J. Yates, Ph.D., University of Illinois at Urbana-Champaign
Felicia Gooler, M.A., University of Illinois at Urbana-Champaign
Deborah Bruns, Ph.D., University of Illinois at Urbana-Champaign

Ty (15 months old) attends a Parents Interacting With Infants (PIWI) group with his mother, Mimi. During a recent parent interview, Mimi told the PIWI facilitators that Ty does not play with anything for longer than "a split second." She worries that he is "hyperactive." She is concerned that Ty will get hurt or not do well in school once he gets old enough to go. She has a hard time keeping up with him, too!

This concern was expressed by several mothers in this parent-child group. But the facilitators also know that children of this age are explorers. They recognize that much of the behavior these parents are concerned about is normal and appropriate. The first step in addressing this concern will be to give these mothers an opportunity to learn more about their children as explorers!

The facilitators planned a PIWI session using the developmental observation topic (DOT), "How I Explore My Environment." They set up the environment with a variety of familiar, age appropriate objects including a Jack-in-the-box, hand puppets, and shape sorters. They also included some unfamiliar objects: a big cardboard box with a door in it, streamers hanging from the ceiling to the floor, and a plastic pool filled with shredded paper. Prior to play time, they asked the parents to think about what their children would do in this environment: Would they dive in and begin exploring, or first sit back and observe? What would their child do with each object? What will they do to help their child find out about the different objects?

Supporting Parents as Developmental Observers

As states increase the number of children and families served, the call for a variety of viable service delivery options becomes paramount. One option to consider is to deliver services through parent-child groups, which maintain the important presence of the parent as a crucial part of the developmental and intervention environment of young children (Browne, Jarrett, Hovey-Lewis, & Freund, 1995). Parent-child groups also provide a context for embedding individualized goals in the natural play activities of young children; provide informal support among parents in a relaxed, natural environment; and foster and enhance developmentally appropriate parent-child interactions.

PIWI (Parents Interacting With Infants) is a relationship-based model for fostering children's development and learning through the medium of parent-child interaction. A key idea underlying how PIWI parent-child group sessions are conducted is that informed observation and interpretation of children's temperament, emotions, and behavior leads to sensitive, responsive interac-  tions between adults and children (Conrad, Gross, Fogg, & Ruchala, 1992; Yates, 1993). These interactions in turn set the stage for optimal development and learning in young children (Bromwich, 1997; Mahoney, Boyce, Fewell, Spiker, & Wheeden, 1998; McCollum & Bair, 1994). For parents of young children with disabilities, the birth to three period may also be a time of learning about and adjusting to their child's special needs. Focused observation highlights the child's competence and the influence of environmental factors, such as activities and materials, on behavior. Through focused observation, parents can gain a greater appreciation of their own role in supporting their child's development. Interaction is enhanced when parents are "tuned into" their child's development. When parents understand behavior from the child's perspective, responsiveness and appropriate support for development are more likely. In PIWI, "developmental observation topics" (DOTs) are the primary means of assisting parents to be developmental observers.

A DOT in Action

Table 1 shows the PIWI session plan for the group session described in the vignette. Evidence of the DOT used to plan this session can be seen throughout the plan as well as in the "topic" line at the top of the plan, and is always a part of the opening discussion, the parent-child interaction/observation time, and the closing discussion. During the opening discussion, the facilitators briefly noted on the session plan some ideas and questions for guiding a conversation about this topic. Evidence of the topic can also be seen in the objects available during discussion time, increasing the chances that while the children are playing they will

Table 1: PIWI Group Session Plan

Date: 6/12   Age Range: 10-30 Months
Developmental Observation Topic: How I Explore My Environment
Observation Focus: What materials keep me interested and engaged?

Schedule	Space/Materials	Group Activities/ Strategies	Individual Strategies*	Team Roles
Greeting (10:00-10:10) Hello Song	on center rug: wooden airplane bead maze puzzles giant shape box Jack-in-the-box dolls with bottles trucks with blocks	Welcome parents & children to the room Focus parents on children's interactions with the materials	Ty: provide favorite objects; be prepared to give individual support Manny: provide favorite truck to entice to central area with other dyads	Sung-Yoon: greet and give name tags; be prepared to follow Ty away from rug if needed Jackie & Felicia on rug with children & parents
Opening Discussion Sharing observation topic (10:10-10:25)	same as above, supplementing with new toys as needed (comment on how children are exploring the toys, which materials they seem interested in, etc.)	Introduce topic: Children are motivated to explore their environments; they explore in different ways. What kinds of materials keep your child interested for long periods of time? (see DOT Plan)	(same as above)	Felicia lead opening discussion Jackie transition toys if needed Sung-Yoon observe children, provide support if needed

* Indicates concerns, interests, or strategies that appear on individual children's IFSPs.   continued

Schedule	Space/Materials	Group Activities/ Strategies	Individual Strategies*	Team Roles
Parent-Child Observation Activities (10:25-10:55)	arranged throughout the room: 1. large box with puppets & vehicles 2. tube box with different size balls & bean bags 3. sock box with little animals & other small objects 4. wooden stairs with streamers hung above 5. water table with bubbles, spoons, strainers, etc. 6. variety of puzzles 7. blocks, trucks	Things to Try: 1. Wait and watch: How does your child explore the materials? 2. Keep your child interested by: a. imitating his/her actions b. adding a new toy to the play c. talking about what your child is doing 3. Watch for persistence and motivation: What is motivating for your child? Which materials are he/she most interested in? Hang "Things to Try" at each activity area	Manny: entice him toward areas where other children are playing* Ty: model "Things to Try" for Mimi to help keep him interested in materials for a longer period of time*	Each facilitator interacts with dyads and provides support for trying the "Things to Try"
Snack (10:55-11:10)	in comfortable location (e.g., snack table): crackers bananas juice or water	ask parents if they have any questions about the group or any issues they want to share with each other	none	Sung-Yoon prepare the snack and facilitate informal discussion Jackie & Felicia remove activity materials
Songs & Games (11:10-11:15)	on center rug: 1. pony song 2. parachute and songs 3. ask if anyone has favorite song or game to share	transition from snack by singing songs	Ty: emphasize pronunciation of "p" and "m" during pony song*	Felicia lead songs Sung-Yoon clean up Jackie participate in songs and games

* Indicates concerns, interests, or strategies that appear on individual children's IFSPs.   continued

Schedule	Space/Materials	Group Activities/ Strategies	Individual Strategies*	Team Roles
Closing Discussion (11:15-11:30)	on center rug: same toys as opening discussion	Ask parents: Which materials were most interesting to your child? What influenced the amount of time your child spent with a material? Different children are motivated by different materials. When opportunities to explore are available, children are more focused and engaged. (See DOT Plan.) Discuss next week's topic.	Ty: provide favorite objects; be prepared to give individual support Manny: provide favorite truck to entice to central area with other dyads	Jackie bring basket of toys to center rug Felicia lead closing discussion Jackie & Sung-Yoon support discussion with observations

* Indicates concerns, interests, or strategies that appear on individual children's IFSPs.

exhibit the exact behaviors that the parents and facilitators are talking about! During the parent-child observation time, the environment has been carefully planned to facilitate parents' observations based on the topic and the focus of the session. A variety of interesting objects are available. Children are free to move and explore, supported by their parents. This is the primary time during which parents observe what their children do, using the opening discussion as a guide. The facilitators move among the parent-child dyads, supporting, commenting, observing, and at times joining in (McCollum & Yates, 1994). They remove or add new materials as needed to keep exploration and interest high. As shown on the session plan, during the closing discussion the parents and facilitators will share what they have observed in relation to the DOT, and the facilitators will provide developmental information to summarize and expand on these observations.

Introduction to DOT Plans

The DOT Plan that provided ideas for this particular session plan is shown in Table 2. The topic for this session was selected in response to concerns and interests expressed by parents in the group. Before the start of this 12-week group the parents were interviewed about what they

Table 2: Developmental Observation Topic (DOT) Plan

Age Range: 10-30 Months

Observation Topic How I Explore My Environment	Observation Focus What materials keep me interested and engaged?
Environment(s) Variety of different types of objects and activities (large, small; familiar, unfamiliar; small/gross motor; water play; etc.); box with puppets & vehicles; tube box with balls & bean bags; sock box; wooden stairs with streamers; water table; puzzles; blocks and trucks	**Things to Try** 1. Wait and watch to see how your child explores the materials 2. Imitate your child's actions 3. Add a new object 4. Talk about what your child is doing 5. Watch to see what types of materials are interesting to your child
Opening Discussion *Introduction:* Children are motivated to explore and conquer (objects and people). Different children explore in different ways and they explore differently when different types of objects are available and when they are comfortable in the situation. By watching what children do and what they practice over and over, we can get a good idea of what they are trying to learn and do. *Questions:* When are your children most active? What do they find most motivating? What keeps them playing for long periods of time? What happens when you add a new angle (object, action) to your child's play? *Predictions:* What materials will your child be most interested in? What will he/she be doing? In which area will your child spend the most time? *Main Points:* When appropriate opportunities for exploring and learning are available, and when the situation is usually comfortable, children usually remain focused and engaged (point out examples using what children are doing during the discussion). Different children are motivated by different types of objects. Adults can help keep children interested by helping them extend what they are doing.	**Closing Discussion** *Predictions:* Were you surprised by where and how long your children played? What went as expected? What didn't? *Questions:* What influenced the amount of time that children spent in one area (novelty of materials, challenging materials, parent strategies)? What strategies did you try to extend your child's play? What worked? *Carry-Over:* What materials does your child most enjoy at home? What materials do you have at home that you could use to help extend his/her play? What strategies might you try at home to help extend your child's play? *Main Points:* When children are not challenged or are challenged too much, they tend to wander in their play. Different children explore differently, and enjoy different kinds of objects. Preferred objects and activities keep children engaged for longer periods than nonpreferred. Children need a stimulating and moderately challenging environment to foster exploration and engagement. Parents can help keep their children interested and channel their high energy level.

hoped to gain from the group for their child and for themselves. A concern with "constant movement" was expressed by several mothers. Thus the facilitators' purpose in selecting the topic "How I Explore My Environment" was to help parents understand this concern within a developmental framework. However, these PIWI facilitators have experience with many different groups, and have developed a file of DOT Plans that reflect commonly expressed interests and concerns.

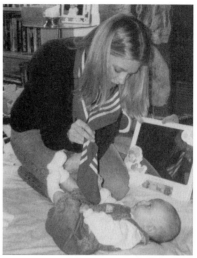

While it is not necessary to have a DOT Plan in order to develop a session plan, DOT Plans can be very helpful and can be reused again and again. The DOT Plans used with a particular group should be carefully selected in response to the interests and concerns expressed by parents during the initial interview or during discussions. As a DOT Plan is translated into a session plan, it is modified based on the individuals in the group. For children with disabilities, individual IFSP goals may also be embedded into the session. For instance, in Ty and Mimi's group, Manny and Ty both have Individualized Family Service Plans (IFSPs), whereas the other children do not. In Table 1, asterisks (*) indicate concerns, interests, and strategies that appear on individual children's IFSPs. For all parents, observation of their own and other children may provide them with a clearer picture of their own child's abilities within a typical play environment. One mother expressed it this way:

> I was interested in learning age appropriate activities. Jake has a lot of developmental delays, especially gross motor delays. [PIWI] renewed my expectations of what he should be doing at different stages.

Some of the topics that these PIWI facilitators have reused many times are shown in Table 3. DOTs are always stated from the child's point of view to remind facilitators and parents that interpreting each child's perspective is an important key to supporting his or her development. Some topics (such as pretend play) are specific to certain developmental ages. Other topics (such as exploration) can be used across a wide range of ages. For example, a birth to four-month old explores by watching, listening, reaching, touching, holding, and moving; a 12- to 18-month old by imitating actions, combining objects, activating switches, using trial and error, and pointing; and a 24- to 36-month old by pretending, using objects as intended, and asking questions. Good DOTs reflect common interests, preferences, and concerns that parents

Table 3: Sample Developmental Observation Topics (DOTs)

Helping adults understand . . .

What I	• Do • Feel • Know	*Why I*	• Try to "do things myself" • Test limits on my behavior
How I	• Explore my environment • Use my senses to learn • Communicate my wants and needs • Show my interest in objects • Express my independence • Pretend • Share with others • Use an adult to help me explore	*How They*	• Support and expand my confidence • Support and expand my competence

have about their children as well as the interests and developmental abilities of the children. DOTs foster acquisition and practice of skills, knowledge, and dispositions appropriate to the developmental ages of the children, and provide materials and activities that facilitate parent participation in children's interests, either through active involvement or through guided observation. Parents enjoy being developmental observers of their children, as described by one mother:

> You set goals for what you would be looking for throughout the [session]. It was more, "Let's see how they [the children] do things" rather than strictly "come here and play." I had an idea of what I was supposed to watch for and do with him.

Developing a DOT Plan

As shown in Table 2, DOT Plans have several sections, all of which are useful in developing the session plan. In addition to the age range and the general observation topic, the DOT Plan also has an observation focus which states a narrower focus of the topic. Writing this focus makes it easier for facilitators to think about the environment that they will provide and open-ended questions to use during the opening and closing discussions. Most important, the focus helps parents to observe by narrowing the range of what they are looking for as they support their child's play. Three different ways of focusing that are especially useful when developing DOTs are: (1) what children do ("What are all of the ways that children ... explore, communicate, move, approach other children, ...?"); (2) the effects of different environments ("What happens when the environment ... contains novel vs. familiar objects, contains large vs. small motor objects, is empty vs. crowded, ...?") ; and (3) the effects of particular adult behavior ("What happens when an adult ... participates vs. sits back, imitates or expands my language, moves me closer to other children ...?).

The same observation topic can be used in many ways, given a different focus. For example, the observation topic "How I Interact With Other Children" could have any one of the following as a focus: how my play is influenced by the types and number of materials available; how I express my interest in others; how I play with children of other ages and genders; or how I play when my parent supports my interactions. Thus, one topic can become many DOT Plans, each with a different focus. A series of sessions on the same topic, but using different DOT Plans, can be especially effective in helping parents investigate an aspect of their children's development in several different ways. The same DOT Plan can also be reused periodically so parents can observe changes in what their children do, know, and feel. Not only is this very reinforcing for parents, it is also a great way for facilitators to collect data on child progress!

Given a well-stated, clear focus, the environment(s) section of the DOT Plan is easy to complete. For example, if the focus is "all of the ways that I explore," the facilitators would include a wide variety of objects appropriate to the developmental age range selected. If the focus is "how I explore novel vs. familiar objects," the DOT Plan would make specific suggestions for novel and familiar objects. "Things to Try" might then include strategies that parents could use to support their children in relation to this focus. For example, to support the focus "how I communicate my wants and needs," parents might try putting materials out

of reach, or sitting on a slide on which the children want to climb.

The opening discussion section includes ideas to prepare parents for observation through sharing what they already know, providing information, and stating how the planned activities will support their observations. During the introduction, facilitators set the context by reminding parents of something that has happened or of a concern related to the topic, and state how this session will address the topic. Open-ended questions help parents think about what their children will do and feel in relation to the topic. Good questions might include, "How does your baby let you know …?" or "What does your child do when …?" The specifics would depend on the particular topic, focus, and environment. The prediction (i.e., taking a guess) further focuses the parents' attention on what they will be observing. After the facilitator shares the environment planned for the day, parents take a guess as to how their child will respond. Guiding questions help parents think about what their child might do: "How do you think your child will respond to …?" or "What do you think your child will like best?" The fourth part of the opening discussion section contains main points that the facilitators can make to summarize the discussion. Main points are brief and build on what the parents already know.

The closing discussion section of the DOT Plan is designed to help parents think about their observations and to link this to what they see their children doing in other contexts. Open-ended questions are used to help parents compare their observations with their earlier predictions, and to think about why they observed what they did (e.g., "What was it about this material that made the children repeatedly go back to it?"). The carry-over section of the Plan includes ideas about what parents could try at home or in the community that would allow similar observations. Finally, ideas are given for main points that can be made about the observation topic, given the particular focus selected. These points are usually very similar to the main points presented in the opening discussion, but now build on what has been observed:

> I liked the discussion because comments that I made were acknowledged, even though the things my kid was doing were different from what someone else's kid was doing. When the facilitator would say, "How do you find your child communicating?" I could express ways that Katie was communicating that might be completely different than theirs, but my answers were still acknowledged.

Summary

Developmental observation topics (DOTs) provide a framework that programs can use for giving parents information about their children's development. The ability to observe and interpret behavior from the perspective of one's child is basic to the sensitivity and responsiveness that underlie developmentally supportive parent-child interaction (Bromwich, 1997; Yates, 1993). Being a good observer brings child development to the forefront of parents' awareness by encouraging them to experience the environment from their child's perspective, reinforcing what they already know about their child's characteristics and behavior. DOTs help parents observe *what* their children do and *why* they do it, and provide a purpose for their own actions as they interact with their child. Individual differences, not developmental status, are the focus, making the activities of the parent-child group interesting and useful to all parents irrespective of their child's age or abilities. DOTs are only one part of the PIWI model, but they are a very important part. As illustrated by the quotations in this article, parents in past PIWI groups have indicated agreement with PIWI goals and have expressed the belief that the goals for the group have been met (McCollum, Gooler, Appl, & Yates, 2001).

Ty and Mimi, like other child-parent dyads in their group, have much to gain from a well-planned, supportive environment that builds on their interactions with one another as a foundation for Ty's development. For Ty, the use of developmental topics can result in opportunities to practice and demonstrate his competence, and expand beyond what he already does, knows, and feels. PIWI provides a setting in which he can gain confidence in his own abilities and in himself as a learner. For Mimi, the developmental observation topic sets a context in which she can experience satisfaction in Ty's competence, understand individual characteristics and environmental factors that influence what Ty does, and develop ideas for what she can do to expand on Ty's experiences. This is also a context in which she can gain confidence and satisfaction in her own role in supporting Ty's development and learning. Developmental observation topics offer a carefully planned, fun way for early interventionists to achieve these important outcomes for infants and toddlers and their families.

Notes

You can reach Jeanette A. McCollum by e-mail at jmccollu@uiuc.edu

The activities described in this article were partially supported by Grant #H029K60102 and Grant #H024D60042 from the Office of Special Education Programs, U.S. Department of Education.

References

Bromwich, R. M. (1997). *Working with families and their infants at risk: A perspective after 20 years of experience.* Austin, TX: Pro-Ed.

Browne, B. C., Jarrett, M. H., Hovey-Lewis, C. J., & Freund, M. B. (1995). *Developmental play group guide.* Tucson, AZ: Communication Skill Builders.

Conrad, B., Gross, D., Fogg, L., & Ruchala, P. (1992). Maternal confidence, knowledge, and quality of mother-infant interactions: A preliminary study. *Infant Mental Health Journal, 13*(4), 353-362.

Mahoney, G., Boyce, G., Fewell, R. R., Spiker, D., & Wheeden, C. A. (1998). The relationship of early intervention services for at-risk children and children with disabilities. *Topics in Early Childhood Special Education*, *18*(1), 5-17.

McCollum, J. A., & Bair, H. (1994). Research in parent-child interaction: Guidance to developmentally appropriate practice for young children with disabilities. In B. L. Mallory & R. S. New (Eds.), *Diversity and developmentally appropriate practices: Challenges for early childhood education* (pp. 84-106). New York: Teachers College Press.

McCollum, J. A., Gooler, F., Appl, D., & Yates, T. J. (2001). PIWI: Enhancing parent-child interaction as a foundation for early intervention. *Infants and Young Children*, *14*(1), 34-45.

McCollum, J. A., & Yates, T. J. (1994). Dyad as focus, triad as means: A family-centered approach to supporting parent-child interactions. *Infants and Young Children*, *6*(4), 54-63.

Yates, T. J. (1993). *Determinants of parent-infant interaction in adolescent mothers.* Dissertation completed in partial fulfillment of the degree in Doctor of Philosophy in Education, University of Illinois, Champaign, IL.

Responsive Conversations: Creating Opportunities for Naturalistic Language Teaching

Ann P. Kaiser, Ph.D., Vanderbilt University
Elizabeth M. Delaney, Ed.D., University of Illinois at Chicago

Conversations between children and their teachers are the anchor for naturalistic teaching and learning in child care and preschool settings. While specific activities and children's immediate interests *define the topic* of the conversation, it is the teacher's skill in scaffolding talk around children, activities, and opportunities for teaching and learning that *creates continuity of conversation*. Through conversations, children learn how to talk, what to talk about, how to respond to a communication partner, how to sustain and extend a topic, and, most important, new information in the natural environment.

The key element of real conversations between children and teachers is *responsive interaction* (Weiss, 1981). Responsive interaction includes a set of strategic behaviors (e.g., following the child's lead, responding to the child's verbal and nonverbal initiations, providing meaningful semantic feedback, expanding the child's utterances) that: (1) maintain the child's interest in the conversation, and (2) provide linguistic models slightly in advance of the child's current language. Responsive interaction is based on developmentally supportive patterns of parent-child interaction and has been shown to be an effective naturalistic language intervention technique for children with autism (Kaiser, Hancock, & Nietfeld, 2000) and children with language delays (Yoder et al., 1995).

Conversations in classrooms require time and teacher focus. Teachers must have techniques for engaging children, extending child participation, and embedding new and functional information in an ongoing exchange. Typical communicative interactions between children and their teachers most often consist of one or two statements by the teacher with one brief response by the child (Kaiser & Hester, 1995). In these exchanges, children may not have sufficient time to respond before teachers shift their attention to another child or activity. Many teacher-child exchanges are adult-directed episodes of instruction giving, didactic teaching, and performance of rote or already known information. While these common exchanges have a place in classroom discourse, such exchanges do not provide rich opportunities for learning in natural contexts.

In this article, we discuss three critical aspects of conversations with children: (1) creating conversations in the classroom; (2) using responsive interaction strategies as a basis for conversations; and (3) embedding naturalistic language prompts in conversations to teach specific skills. Figure 1 provides a schematic of these elements. Our discussion is based on research in early language intervention including studies with parents and teachers (Barnard, 1997; Delaney & Kaiser, 2001; Fey, 1986).

Figure 1: Enhanced Milieu Teaching

Creating Conversations

Space for adults and children to have meaningful conversations requires planning the daily classroom schedule to allow time for one-to-one interactions. Activities during centers, small group times, outdoor play, and free play must be selected or arranged so that the group of children can sustain their participation without continuous teacher input. Then, when most children are engaged and participating independently, the teacher has brief conversations with individual children. Planning for independence, scheduling specific times for conversations with children, and monitoring the actual occurrence of individual conversations may be necessary to ensure that adult-child conversations happen. Even with planning, time for talk with individual children will be limited in a group care setting. Thus, it is essential that adults are able to quickly and effectively join children in their "conversational space."

Table 1 summarizes five steps for creating a conversation. First, join the child in his or her "space." Sit at the child's level and make eye contact or nonverbally establish a connection with the child. By smiling, gently touching the child, or offering related materials, you communicate your attention to the child's activity without shifting the child's focus away from the activity. Second, it is important to spend a few

Table 1: Creating Conversations With Young Children

1. Sit near the child at eye level; establish visual and physical contact.

2. Watch what the child is doing and notice what he or she is communicating.

3. Follow the child's agenda.

4. Relate your materials to the child's materials.

5. Expand the child's play.

seconds watching the child's activity before beginning to talk. Watching the child's activity and nonverbal communication provides a topic for conversation and indicates points of entry into the child's conversational space.

Third, follow the child's activity agenda. Begin by commenting to the child about what is happening, rather than by asking questions. Positive descriptions of child activities demonstrate interest in the child and his or her activity without being overly intrusive. Positive affect and a playful style signal to the child that you are available for talk and interaction. Take your cues from the child. If the child resists an approach or does not want you to join his or her play at this time, then pull back and wait for a better opportunity for conversation.

Fourth, if the child is open to your approach, use parallel materials to enter the interaction (conversation). Begin by placing materials next to the child's and imitating his or her actions. For example, build a similar tower, draw the same picture, or pat dough using the same rhythm. Next, invite the child to exchange materials or join in the child's activity. You might join a child's activity by taking turns placing blocks on a single tower, drawing on the same paper, or giving the child more dough as he or she needs some.

Fifth, as play with the child becomes more interactive, describe exactly what the child is doing and elaborate on the child's play theme. For example, if the child is making snakes with dough, you could provide dough for additional animals, comment on individual animals, or group and label them for the child:

Child: Rolls clay into a snake.

Adult: "You made a snake. It is so-oo long."
Adult: Hands child more dough and waits.
Child: Makes another snake. "Snake."
Adult: "Another snake. It's a fat snake."
Adult: Hands child more dough and waits.
Child: Makes another snake. "More snakes."
Adult: "One, two, three snakes. You made three green snakes."

Adult comments should be descriptive, rather than directive. Direct commands or instructions shift control to the adult and away from the child resulting in an unbalanced interaction. The goal is to follow the child's lead and begin a conversation around the child's immediate interests.

If the child responds to adult comments by making a verbal response or by incorporating the suggestions into his or her play, the adult can expand the child's utterance or play to continue the conversation. Giving the child new materials or demonstrating a new use of materials can further extend the interaction:

Child: Rolls dough into a snake, and then uses a cookie cutter
         to make a rabbit.
Adult: "You made a snake and a rabbit. (Pause.) We could have
         a zoo for your animals."
Child: "OK, zoo."
Adult: Places blocks around the snake. "I made a cage for
         the snake."
Adult: Hands child more blocks.
Child: Places blocks around rabbit. "I made it."
Adult: "You built a rabbit cage!"

Using Responsive Interaction Strategies

Once the adult and child have entered an interaction in which the adult is attending to the child's activities in a positive, nondirective manner, the adult can scaffold the child's participation into meaningful, age appropriate conversations. *Responsive interaction (RI)* strategies can be used to simultaneously engage the child in conversation and to support the language development of children with communication and speech disorders (McLean & Woods-Cripe, 1997). RI strategies are key adult behaviors in conversation-based naturalistic teaching (Kaiser, Hancock, & Hester, 1998; Weiss, 1981). Table 2 lists RI strategies that can be incorporated into a conversation and the rationale for their use (discussed next). Table 3 is an example of an adult-child conversation illustrating how RI strategies can be used to engage a child in conversation

Table 2: Responsive Interaction Strategies

Adult Skill	Rationale
1. Balance verbal and nonverbal adult-child turns.	Creates a conversational framework for interaction; establishes child's equitable role in interaction
2. Pause after each adult utterance.	Encourages child-initiated utterances; maintains balance of turns
3. Respond verbally to nonverbal behavior.	Informs the child that the adult is attending to the child's activities; bridges child actions to words
4. Give semantic feedback to child language.	Meaningful, related responses encourage child communication and provide context-specific language models
5. Model language about what the adult and child are doing.	Maps context and anchors to introduce specific language forms
6. Ask a limited number of real questions.	Small numbers of adult real questions maintain balance in the interactions and allow the child to give longer and more meaningful responses
7. Expand child utterances.	Lets the child know that the adult heard and understood the utterance while simultaneously modeling more sophisticated language forms and continuing topic
8. Decrease the frequency of instructions.	Giving commands only for "important" behaviors increases child compliance and maintains balance in the conversation

and concurrently support language development. In this example, the adult and child have a similar number of turns (RI strategy #1). The adult asks questions only to clarify the child's meaning (RI strategy #6). The tone of the conversation is playful. The adult responds to each child comment with a meaningful, closely related comment (RI strategy #4) or an expansion of the child's utterance (RI strategy #7). Strategic pauses allow the child time to process the information and formulate an appropriate response (RI strategy #2). Pausing for three to five seconds after each turn also helps the adult match the frequency and length of the child's turns and allows the child to set the pace of the conversation (RI strategy #1).

Modeling New Language in Conversations

One of the most important functions of conversations with children is providing models for new language in a meaningful, everyday context. RI strategies are an ideal way to model new language in conversations. Children learn new vocabulary when adults: (1) label objects and events,

Table 3: Using Responsive Interaction to Model Language and Extend Conversation

An adult and a child are side-by-side in front of a child-sized table, drawing with crayons on two large sheets of paper. The adult sometimes turns to look at the child when she talks. The child sits in a rocking chair; the adult sits on the floor at about the same height as the child.

Child: Points to the letter "P" written on the paper.
Adult: "P for pizza." [Describes the child's nonverbal behavior]
Pause.
Child: "Yeah."
Adult: "I love pizza." [Semantic feedback; models language about the topic]
Child: "OK."
Adult: "With pepperoni." [Semantic feedback; models language about the topic]
Pause.
Child: "And with chocolate."
Adult: "Chocolate pizza?!" [Real question about child's meaning]
Child: "Chocolate ice cream."
Adult: "Chocolate ice cream with a cherry on top." [Expansion of child's utterance]
Pause.
Child: "And a chocolate, with uh, with strawberries on it."
Adult: "Chocolate ice cream with chocolate sauce and strawberries." [Expansion of child utterance]
Pause.
Child: "And chocolate."
Adult: "Mmm, I like vanilla." [Semantic feedback; continues conversation]
Child: "Vanilla with ... "
Pause.
Adult: "Vanilla ice cream." [Expansion of child's utterance]
Child: "With chocolate."
Adult: "With chocolate sauce." [Expansion of child's utterance]
Child: "And ... "
Pause.
Adult: "And whipped cream." [Expansion of child utterance]
Child: "Whipped cream."
Adult: "I love whipped cream." [Semantic feedback; continues conversation]
Adult: "Hey Dawn, thanks for sitting with me and coloring." [Praise; describes child behavior]
Child: "I'm, I'm rocking."
Adult: "You're rocking and you're writing." [Expansion of child utterance]
Child: "Mmm." Hums tune sung earlier in the day.
Adult: "And you're singing!" [Semantic feedback; describes child behavior]

(2) specifically describe actions, and (3) replace general pronouns (e.g., it, there, that) with specific labels for objects, people, and places. When the adult follows the child's play agenda, there are many opportunities to label the child's play materials and actions and to use those labels consistently throughout the conversation. For example, when you join a

child at the water table, label the materials (e.g., water wheel, bucket, sponge, cups, and soap) and describe the child's actions to introduce verbs (e.g., pouring, squeezing, filling, and washing).

Child: Pours water on water
         wheel.
Adult: "Pour water." (adult
         pours)
Child: "Water." (child
         pours)
Adult: "Pour water." (adult
         pours)
Child: "Water again!" (child
         pours)
Adult: "Pour water again!"
         (adult pours)

Using the same labels throughout the conversation gives the child with limited language several opportunities to hear the word in context. Although modeling should always follow the child's immediate actions and interests, lesson planning can enhance effective modeling. Preparing lists of vocabulary words (nouns, verbs, adjectives, prepositions) and short phrases (two-, three-, and four-word utterances) that can be used to describe a particular activity and storing these lists with the activity materials supports "spontaneous" modeling in a busy classroom.

Adult-child conversations also offer opportunities to teach elaborated phrases and sentences. As adults extend conversations around a child's theme, they can model elaborated language forms by: (1) reformulating, or (2) expanding on the child's utterance (RI strategy #7), (3) descriptively praising child behavior (RI strategy #3), and (4) describing the child and other actions (RI strategy #5). First, reformulate the child's sentence by adding to or specifying a noun or verb phrase:

Child: "I paint tree."
Adult: "You *painted* a tree!"

Reformulations simultaneously maintain the semantic topic of the child's utterance and demonstrate correct grammatical structure (Farrar, 1990). Second, expand the child's utterance to more fully describe his or her action and intention:

Child: "Car fall!"
Adult: "The car fell *off the table*!"

Expansions connect the child's existing language with additional semantic information. Often, the child will spontaneously imitate expansions or use the new information later in the conversation. Third, model new language forms by descriptively praising the child's behavior (e.g., "You *painted a beautiful car*" or "Thank you for *stacking the blocks on the shelf*"). Adult praise is powerful and attractive to most children. Verbal praise given immediately following a child behavior reinforces the positive social aspects of the action as it models more complex language forms. Fourth, give a description of a parallel action to model new language forms (e.g., "Your friend Kristin is feeding her baby, too"). Parallel descriptions connect the child's behavior to other people or related activities. Descriptions of parallel action can also be used to bring another child into the play sequence and encourage child-to-child conversations.

Another strategy is to ask a real question (RI strategy #6) to obtain new information and create an opportunity to model language in response to the child's utterance. Choose questions carefully. Open-ended questions used sparingly will support conversation, and encourage children to use longer, more specific utterances. Questions like, "What else will you paint?" or "What animals will visit your tree?" encourage specific vocabulary use by children. Yes/no questions (e.g., "Will you paint another tree?") and "test" questions (e.g., "What color are the branches?") often yield single-word responses. For a child with limited language skills, yes/no and test questions may end the conversation prematurely unless the adult scaffolds the child's response into the conversation and elicits additional elaboration.

Using Prompts to Teach Language in Conversation

Language prompts such as *models*, *mand-models*, and *time delays* are naturalistic strategies that have been demonstrated to be effective in teaching new communication skills (Hemmeter & Kaiser, 1994; Kaiser, 1998). The key to using prompting strategies in conversation is to teach only when the child is interested and motivated to respond to the prompt. It is easiest to teach when the child is requesting; however, there may be relatively few opportunities to teach to requests without disrupting the flow of the conversation. Choose those opportunities that have an obvious positive consequence (i.e., a child-specified reinforcer) and make both the prompt and the consequence as natural as possible. Naturalistic teaching episodes typically contain only two prompts (an initial prompt and a follow-up prompt if the child does not respond or responds incorrectly) in order to maintain the flow of conversation. If the child loses interest, the teaching opportunity is over; transition to the child's new topic.

Elicitive modeling is used when a child has not yet acquired independent production of a language form. After establishing joint attention focused on an object or activity, the teacher presents a verbal model directly related to the child's behavior. If the child correctly imitates the model after the first or second attempt, the teacher gives the child immediate positive feedback:

Child: Reaches for baby bottle. [Child request]
Adult: "Say, 'I want bottle.'" [Model]
Child: "Want bottle."
Adult: "I want bottle." [Corrective model]
Child: "I want bottle."
Adult: Gives child the bottle. [Feedback and compliance with child request] "Yes, here is the bottle for your baby!"

If the child does not correctly imitate the language model, the teacher restates the language model and continues on with play and conversation:

Child: Reaches for baby bottle.
Adult: "Say, 'I want bottle.'" [Model]
Child: "Bottle."
Adult: "I want bottle." [Corrective model]
Child: "Bottle."
Adult: "You want the bottle." Gives child the bottle. [Feedback and compliance with child request]

The mand-model procedure (Rogers-Warren & Warren, 1980) differs from modeling by including a nonimitative verbal prompt in the form of a question (e.g., "What do you want?"), a choice (e.g., "Do you want the bottle or the spoon?"), or a mand (e.g., "Tell me what you want"). The key to the effective use of mands is creating an opportunity for the child to make real choices. If the child responds correctly, immediate reinforcement follows. If the child does not respond to the mand, the adult provides a model:

Adult: Do you want a fork or a spoon? [Choice mand]
Child: Reaches for spoon.
Adult: "Say, 'I want the spoon.'" [Model]
Child: "Spoon."
Adult: "Say, 'I want the spoon.'" [Corrective model]

Child: "Spoon."
Adult: "You want the spoon." Gives child the spoon. [Feedback and compliance with child request]

The time delay procedure (Halle, Baer, & Spradlin, 1981) is used to teach children to respond to the nonverbal environmental cues for communication. When using a time delay, the teacher pauses when the child nonverbally signals his or her communicative intent. If the child fills the pause by verbally communicating, the teacher responds to the communication attempt. If the child does not verbalize, the teacher provides a model to further support a child verbalization:

Adult: Holds a basket filled with small toys where the child can see it, but cannot reach it, for three seconds. [Time delay]
Child: Reaches for toys.
Adult: "Say, 'toys.'" [Model]
Child: "Toys."
Adult: "Here are toys for you." Gives the child toys and continues play. [Feedback and compliance with child request]

Effective naturalistic prompting does not disrupt the communicative flow between the adult and the child. The conversation continues and quickly moves from prompted or supported communication to other child initiations and responses. There should be no more than one prompt during 15-20 conversational turns between the adult and child. Communication and continued conversation are the primary goals; prompting specific language is a secondary goal.

Conclusion

Conversations are a form of advanced social interaction between teachers and children. Creating a space for conversation in the classroom is an investment to support children's learning, particularly their language learning. Teachers create spaces for conversations by allocating their physical and verbal attention to extended interactions that follow a child's interests and activity. Using responsive interaction strategies sustains child engagement in conversation and models diverse vocabulary and complex new language in context. Embedding occasional, highly functional prompts for language use into conversations teaches children to produce language in context.

Notes

You can reach Ann P. Kaiser by e-mail at ann.kaiser@vanderbilt.edu

Preparation of this article was funded in part by grants from the Administration on Families, Youth, and Children's Head Start Mental Health Partnerships Program (90YM002) and the National Institute of Mental Health (R01MH54629).

References

Barnard, K. E. (1997). Influencing parent-child interactions for children at-risk. In M. J. Guralnick (Ed.), *The effectiveness of early intervention* (pp. 249-268). Baltimore: Paul H. Brookes.

Delaney, E. M., & Kaiser, A. P. (2001). The effects of teaching parents blended communication and behavior support strategies. *Behavioral Disorders, 26*(2), 93-116.

Farrar, M. J. (1990). Discourse and the acquisition of grammatical morphemes. *Journal of Child Language, 17*(3), 607-624.

Fey, M. E. (1986). *Language intervention with young children.* Boston: Allyn and Bacon.

Halle, J. W., Baer, D. M., & Spradlin, J. E. (1981). Teachers' generalized use of delay as a stimulus control procedure to increase language use in handicapped children. *Journal of Applied Behavior Analysis, 14*(4), 387-400.

Hemmeter, M. L., & Kaiser, A. P. (1994). Enhanced milieu teaching: Effects of parent-implemented language intervention. *Journal of Early Intervention, 18*(3), 269-289.

Kaiser, A. P. (1998). Teaching functional communication skills. In M. E. Snell (Ed.), *Instruction of students with severe disabilities* (5th ed.) (pp. 453-492). New York: Macmillan.

Kaiser, A. P., Hancock, T. B., & Nietfeld, J. P. (2000). The effects of parent-implemented enhanced milieu teaching on the social communication of children who have autism. *Journal of Early Education and Development, 11*(4), 423-446.

Kaiser, A. P., & Hester, P. P. (1995). How everyday environments support children's communication. In L. K. Koegel, R. L. Koegel, & G. Dunlap (Eds.), *Positive behavioral support* (pp. 145-162). Baltimore: Paul H. Brookes.

McLean, L. K., & Woods-Cripe, J. (1997). The effectiveness of early intervention for children with communication disorders. In M. J. Guralnick (Ed.), *The effectiveness of early intervention* (pp. 349-428). Baltimore: Paul H. Brookes.

Rogers-Warren, A. K., & Warren, S. F. (1980). Mands for verbalizations: Facilitating the display of newly trained language in children. *Behavior Modifications, 4*(2), 361-382.

Weiss, R. S. (1981). INREAL intervention for language handicapped and bilingual children. *Journal of the Division for Early Childhood, 4*(1), 40-52.

Yoder, P. J., Kaiser, A. P., Goldstein, H., Alpert, C., Mousetis, L., Kaczmarek, L., & Fischer, R. (1995). A comparison of milieu teaching and responsive interaction in classroom applications. *Journal of Behavioral Education, 19*(3), 151-171.

Facilitating the Development of Intentional Communication

Rebecca B. McCathren, Ph.D., University of Missouri
Amy L. Watson, B.S., University of Missouri

One of the most important developmental milestones that occurs during the early years of life is the transition from unintentionally communicating basic needs to intentionally communicating with a partner. When children become intentional communicators they can engage in increasingly more complicated social interactions. These interactions are critical to cognitive and social-emotional development. This transition increases the child's mastery of the environment and also increases his or her ability to interpret the communication acts of others, both of which are essential to learning important cause and effect relationships, making meaning of events and objects in the environment, and engaging in more sophisticated patterns of play behavior (Bloom, 1993). Most important, however, this transition signifies children's understanding that their behavior has an effect on the important people in their lives. Without this basic understanding, children cannot develop the ability to use meaningful patterns of communication with others, including speech, sign language, or alternative symbolic communication systems (Bloom, 1993). For many children with special needs this critical transition is delayed, or does not occur at all, inhibiting the development of language.

A transactional model of development (Wetherby, Warren, & Reichle, 1998) provides the theoretical underpinnings for this article. In a transactional model the child and environment have a reciprocal effect on each other. Changes in the child cause caregivers to respond differently, which supports further changes in development.

How Young Children Become Intentional Communicators

Preintentional Prelinguistic Communication

Three-month old Tamika starts to squirm and make short plaintive cries. Her father notices and says, "Oh, you must be getting hungry," and feeds her a bottle. The behavior of infants is in response to internal states and without intent to affect the world. The behavior of infants is only communicative because there are adults in their environment who interpret their behavior and respond to it. Tamika did not fuss in order to prompt her father to feed her. Rather, she fussed because she felt uncomfortable.

This earliest stage of communication is referred to as perlocutionary (Bates, 1976), or can be described as *preintentional prelinguistic* communication. The communication is preintentional because it is not yet used with the intent to communicate, and is prelinguistic because it develops prior to the development of language (i.e., words). When infants are in this stage of development adults tend to talk to them in long verbal strings that communicate positive regard. The words are much less important than the prosody of the speech, the emotional match between adult and infant, and the feelings being communicated.

Six-month old Michael's cracker falls off his high chair to the floor. He looks at it and reaches for it, vocalizing, "na-na-na." His mother sees the cracker on the floor and retrieves it for him. Michael's behaviors are still considered preintentional because they focus on an interesting object or event without including a communication partner. An infant in this stage of development may vocalize and reach toward an out of reach object, but would not engage in any behaviors with the intent of having an adult retrieve the object.

Making the Transition From Preintentional to Intentional Communication

Nine-month old Juan sees his bottle but can not reach it. He reaches toward the bottle, then looks at his father and vocalizes, "ba-duh-duh" until his father gives him the bottle. Eleven-month old Sarah hears a siren outside and points to the direction of the sound, alternating

her gaze between where she is pointing and her mother, until her mother comments, "That's a fire engine out there; it's noisy." There is a new component in these children's communication acts that was absent from the communication acts in the previous examples. These children now include the adults in their communication acts

and demonstrate an intent to communicate to the adults. At about nine or ten months of age, infants who are typically developing begin to demonstrate communication skills that mark the transition from preintentional to *intentional* communication.

Intentionality is demonstrated by the use of coordinated attention. Coordinated attention is a child's ability to alternately gaze between the object or event that is the focus of the communication and the adult. An added feature of intentionality is persistence. The child will typically persist with the behavior until either the demand is satisfied or it becomes clear that the demand will not be satisfied.

Adult Behavior That Facilitates Language Development

When infants become intentional communicators adults tend to respond in ways that facilitate language development. Adults begin to talk in shorter sentences and to use concrete words and highly redundant language that has been labeled as "parentese" (also referred to as "motherese," since most of the research on this child-directed speech has focused on mothers). One of the most important features of parentese is adult linguistic mapping, or using precise vocabulary to say what the child is communicating. For example, Maddie hears a dog barking, runs to the window, and alternates her gaze between the dog and her father. Her father says, "That's a dog. What a noisy dog." The next stage in communication development is the *linguistic* stage, occurring when children use words or other symbolic representations to label objects and actions.

For toddlers with disabilities that interfere with or delay the development of intentionality, that communication dance between adult and child may not happen in the same way. Sometimes children with developmental delays do not engage or engage infrequently in the communication behaviors that "turn on" parentese in adults (Warren & Yoder, 1998). In these cases, language development can be facilitated by targeting the specific skills that are the precursors of intentional communication and have been demonstrated to predict later language abilities.

Prelinguistic Milieu Teaching

One intervention that has been developed specifically to facilitate the transition to intentional communication in young children is Prelinguistic Milieu Teaching (PMT) (Warren, Yoder, Gazdag, Kim, & Jones, 1993). This intervention is based on a milieu language teaching model (Kaiser, Yoder, & Keetz, 1992) and has been adapted for use with prelinguistic children who have, or are at risk for, language delays. This intervention encompasses a number of teaching strategies that target specific behaviors that have been shown to be the precursors of intentional communication. The goal of PMT is to teach children to become intentional communicators who communicate more frequently and with greater clarity, thereby providing adults with more opportunities to respond in ways that enhance further development.

The strategies are employed in a naturalistic setting, in various activities, and in response to the child's interests and actions. Young children are more likely to acquire new skills when they are actively engaged in an activity, skills are taught using the materials and activities a child is attending to, and teaching occurs in the environment where the child needs those skills (Bricker, Pretti-Frontczak, McComas, 1998; Linder, 1993). These strategies have been successfully used by parents (Wilcox, 1992) and teachers (McCathren, 2000), and with children with a variety of disabilities (Yoder & Warren, 1999).

Pragmatic Functions

Intentional communication is used for a variety of purposes. These different social uses of communication are known as pragmatic functions. Bruner (1981) identified three categories of pragmatic functions of communication that develop in the first year: (1) behavioral regulation or requesting, or controlling another's behavior to get them to perform an action (e.g., give a bottle, manipulate a toy); (2) social interaction, or getting another's attention for social purposes (e.g., playing peek-a-boo, showing off); and (3) joint attention or commenting, or directing another's attention in order to establish a shared focus on an activity, object, or person. The exact age and order of onset for these three pragmatic skills varies across children (Carpenter, Mastergeorge, & Coggins, 1983).

PMT is used to teach requesting and commenting to young children who are infrequent intentional communicators. Requesting (Mundy, Kasari, Sigman, & Ruskin, 1995; Smith & vonTetzchner; 1986) and commenting (McCathren, Yoder, & Warren, 1999; Mundy et al., 1995; Mundy, Sigman, & Kasari, 1990) have predicted language outcomes for children who are typically developing and those with delays or disabilities. These are typically the earliest types of interactions in which intentionality is demonstrated by young children (Bates, O'Connell, & Shore, 1987) and also are the most commonly occurring pragmatic functions in the prelinguistic period (Wetherby, Cain, Yonclas, & Walker, 1988).

PMT Strategies

Young children use a combination of vocalizations, gestures, and coordinated attention to request and establish joint attention. PMT strategies are designed to facilitate the use of these behaviors. Warren and Yoder (1998) have identified a set of procedures they have termed "enabling contexts" (p. 372). The enabling contexts include following the child's lead, environmental arrangement, and establishing turn-taking.

Enabling Contexts

Following the Child's Lead. One of the first strategies of many communication interventions is to focus the interaction on the object or event the child is attending to. Many studies have shown that communication development is enhanced when adults label, ask questions, or give directives that match the child's topic (McCathren, Yoder, & Warren, 1995). One way to self-monitor how often we communicate in ways that do not follow a child's lead is to become aware of how often we say "look" or "watch" in attempts to direct and change a child's focus of attention.

Following the child's attentional lead includes two main verbal strategies: linguistic mapping and descriptive talk. Linguistic mapping is when the adult uses words for what the child is communicating. For example, if the child startles at a loud noise and looks frightened, the adult might put her hands over her ears and say, "That's loud." Or, if a child shakes a jar in an attempt to get it open, the adult might say, "You want it open." Descriptive talk uses exact vocabulary to describe what the child is doing. While a child is playing, the adult might provide descriptive comments on what they are doing or playing with. For example, when a child is playing with a truck, the adult uses brief and concrete descriptions such as "you push truck," "red truck," or "truck goes fast."

Environmental Arrangement. Environmental arrangement is used to create opportunities and the need for young children to communicate (Ostrosky & Kaiser, 1991). Thinking about how the environment is set up is important because children are most likely to initiate about things they want, need, or find interesting (Warren & Yoder, 1998). Environmental arrangement strategies are used to encourage children to communicate to request a toy or activity, one of the important pragmatic functions targeted in PMT. One of the environmental arrangements includes placing things the child wants (e.g., food or toys) in places the child cannot access independently (Ostrosky & Kaiser, 1991; Warren & Yoder, 1998). This strategy is only successful if the adult has been able to identify what toys, foods, or activities each child prefers. Parents can be enormously helpful in identifying high preference toys or objects. Once high preference items are identified they can be placed in transparent containers with tight lids so the child can see them but cannot get them out. They also can be put on shelves so they are in view, but out of the child's reach. Another strategy is to have high preference toys or activities that the child needs help to use (e.g., bubbles, toys with difficult switches).

Joint attention is also taught through environmental arrangement. Children use joint attention to get adults to look at what they are noticing (Warren & Yoder, 1998). The strategies for this are to take advantage of all the "distracters" in the environment. Loud noises, interruptions, and unexpected events can all be used to teach joint attention. If the environment does not provide those opportunities the adult can plan these events. Initially the adult will model joint attention. For example, as a spider walks across the floor, the adult points at the spider, looks at the child, and says "spider." Once the child is able to imitate the point, vocalization, and eye contact the adult might ignore an event and wait for the child to recruit his or her attention (Warren & Yoder, 1998).

Developing Turn-Taking Routines. Another strategy is to develop a routine (e.g., blowing bubbles) and then violate the routine by either not taking a turn, or by doing something silly or unexpected that prompts the child to direct the adult to continue. The adult can use prompts, time delays, and models to encourage the use of communicative behaviors by the child (e.g., eye contact, gaze shift, vocalizations, and conventional gestures). Like the use of environmental arrangement, this strategy teaches children to use communication to regulate others' behaviors. For example, Susan and her mother are rolling a ball back and forth, a new skill that they have been working on for several weeks. One day, instead of rolling the ball back, Susan's mother waits. After Susan looks at her and vocalizes, "ba," her mother rolls the ball back to her. If Susan did not respond to her mother simply holding the ball or was frustrated by her mother's delay, her mother might have tried doing some-

thing silly, like holding the ball on her head or behind her back.

Teaching Strategies

In addition to enabling contexts, PMT uses a number of specific strategies to facilitate the development of frequent and clear intentional communication. Specific strategies are used to facilitate the child's use of coordinated attention, vocalization, and gestures. The strategies used to teach these include vocal and behavioral imitation and developing turn-taking, modeling conventional gestures, and prompting for communication. The strategies are not necessarily practiced in a specific sequence, but are used when they can most optimally be incorporated into an activity (see Table 1).

Imitation and Turn-Taking. Behaviors that are consistent with following the child's lead are physical imitation or mirroring (Kaiser, 1993b) and vocal imitation (Warren et al., 1993). Imitation is one way to ensure that the adult is following the child's lead and it also lets the child regulate the content and pacing of the interaction (Warren & Yoder, 1998). Physical imitation is especially useful as a way to develop turn-taking and play routines. The adult can insert a short, imitated turn into the child's play. Once this is established the adult can begin to modify his or her turns and begin to build and elaborate on play routines. For example, the child is banging Play-Doh™ with her fist. A typical reaction of an adult is to try to get the child to "make something" or to be more constructive in the play (e.g., "Let's roll it out. Can you make a snake?"). However, in this model the adult might say, "My turn" and bang the child's Play-Doh™ or bang on her Play-Doh™ matching the speed and intensity of the child. After a few rounds of imitation the adult can slightly alter the play (e.g., hitting with an open hand or pushing on the Play-Doh™). If the child changes her action to match the adult's, a new game begins. If the child does not follow, the adult should immediately go back to imitating the child.

Table 1: Incorporating PMT Strategies Into Daily Activities

Activity	Teaching Strategies	Child's Behavior	Adult's Response
Sensory Table	Physical Imitation	Austin dumps sand out of a cup	Ms. Hazel dumps sand out of another cup
	Physical Imitation and Vocal Imitation	Austin pushes his hands into the sand and says "uh"	Ms. Hazel pushes her hand into the sand and says "uh"
	Vocal Model	Austin is sitting idle	Ms. Hazel pours sand from her hand and says "ma"
Free Play	Physical Imitation Paired With a Vocal Model	Austin pours sand into a water wheel	Ms. Hazel pours sand into the water wheel and says "da-da-da"
	Descriptive Talk	Austin continues rolling a truck	Ms. Hazel says "roll the truck," "red truck," and "vroom"
Play-Doh™	Prompting for Eye Contact (Time Delay)	Austin tries to open the jar of Play-Doh™	Ms. Hazel pauses and looks expectantly for Austin to make eye contact with her
	Linguistic Mapping	Austin pushes the Play-Doh™ to Ms. Hazel and looks at her	Ms. Hazel opens the jar and says, "Want Play-Doh™"
	Gesture Model	Austin watches a maintenance person who enters the room	Ms. Hazel points and says, "There's Joe!"
Snack Time	Physical Imitation and Vocal Model	Austin chews crackers	Ms. Hazel pretends to chew and says, "mmhh"
	Prompting for Eye Contact	Austin reaches for the box of crackers	Ms. Hazel holds the box close to her face and waits for Austin to make eye contact
	Linguistic Mapping	Austin looks at Ms. Hazel	Ms. Hazel gives Austin more crackers and says, "More cracker"

Vocal imitation also encourages turn-taking and helps develop a vocal back-and-forth format, which is a precursor to verbal conversation. For example, Susan and her teacher are banging on drums. While banging on her drum, Susan says, "da-da" and her teacher imitates her by saying, "da-da."

Modeling Vocalizations and Gestures. In addition to imitating vocalizations, an adult may also model vocalizations that contain consonants. This is particularly important for children who rarely vocalize and therefore provide few opportunities for imitation. For example, Jonathan and his mother are playing with sand. His mother drops sand from her hand while saying, "ba-ba-ba." Pairing vocal models with physical imitation may encourage a child to use more complex and frequent vocalizations during play. For example, when Jonathan pushes his fingers into the sand, his mother can imitate by pushing her fingers into the sand while adding the vocalization "da." In many cases, an adult may feel uncomfortable making sounds typically associated with infant babbling while playing with an older child. However, it is important to remember that the speech sounds children typically use most frequently—[m], [b], and [d]—serve as a bridge to their first words (Stoel-Gammon, 1998).

Adults can also model conventional gestures. Conventional gestures include pointing to out of reach objects or events, shrugging one's shoulders, upturning the palms, nodding or shaking the head to indicate yes or no, waving, and making the "shhh" gesture. For example, Austin and his teacher are taking turns stacking blocks to make a tower. The block building falls over. Ms. Hazel points to the blocks and says, "uh-oh."

Prompting for Eye Contact. One of the frequently missing behavioral components in a prelinguistic child's communication is eye contact with a partner. Before verbally prompting for eye contact an adult may use two less intrusive strategies. The first strategy is to intersect the child's gaze by positioning the adult's face at the child's eye level and bringing an interesting object close to the adult's eyes. This can result in the child "accidentally" making eye contact. Time delays (Kaiser, 1993a) can also be used to elicit eye contact from the child (Warren & Yoder, 1998). For example, Ms. Hazel and Austin have developed a routine in which Austin touches pictures in a book and Ms. Hazel names the picture. However, Austin does not make eye contact as part of the book reading routine. When Austin points to the picture, Ms. Hazel can wait for him to make eye contact before naming the picture. If intersecting the child's gaze and time delays are not successful in eliciting eye contact the adult may use a verbal prompt. For example, Austin wants the doll that is in a closed container, and repeatedly shakes the container. Ms. Hazel takes the container and waits. Austin does not look at Ms. Hazel, so she prompts, "Look at me." Note that it is important to use prompts sparingly and to never withhold the requested object indefinitely. If Austin does not look at Ms. Hazel, she will eventually get the doll out of the container and continue playing. Interactions should be playful and enjoyable for both children and the adults.

Once children are frequent intentional communicators parents and teachers can focus on teaching symbolic skills using speech, signs, pictures, or other alternative systems. Instead of modeling vocalizations and gestures adults can model words and signs, or can implement whatever communication system has been identified for a particular child.

Summary

In conclusion, PMT strategies can be used by parents and caregivers to facilitate the communication development of young children. Some of the strategies (e.g., modeling and imitating vocalizations and gestures, following the child's lead) can be done virtually anywhere. Other strategies (e.g., environmental arrangement) may require more planning to use successfully. However, all of the strategies can be embedded into the typical daily routines of young children.

How PMT is implemented will vary slightly from child to child. Because PMT uses mutual engagement in activities as the context for intervention, it is important to use toys, activities, or snacks that the child responds to and finds rewarding. For some children, it may require careful observation to discover these motivations.

Some adults may think they do not have enough time to devote individual attention to any one child long enough to engage in these routines. However, these strategies can be done in short teaching episodes throughout the day by taking advantage of opportunities that arise that necessitate communicative exchanges. It is not necessary, or probably even desirable, to do intensive intervention for long periods of time. Interspersing intervention into daily routines will help children learn to communicate at times when communication is most effective.

Finally, a key element to this intervention is to establish a comfortable, playful interaction. When the intervention is being conducted successfully, both partners are relaxed, happy, and having fun.

Note
You can reach Rebecca B. McCathren by e-mail at McCathrenR@missouri.edu

References
Bates, E. (1976). *Language and context: The acquisition of pragmatics.* New York: Academic Press.
Bates, E., O'Connell, B., & Shore, C. (1987). Language and communication in infancy. In J. Osofsky (Ed.), *Handbook of infant development* (pp. 149-203). New York: Wiley & Sons.
Bloom, L. (1993). *The transition from infancy to language: Acquiring the power of expression* (pp. 3-20). Melbourne, Australia: Cambridge University Press.
Bricker, D., Pretti-Frontczak, K., & McComas, N. (1998). *An activity-based approach to early intervention: Second edition* (pp. 7-21). Baltimore: Paul H. Brookes.
Bruner, J. (1981). The social context of language acquisition. *Language and Communication, 1,* 155-178.
Carpenter, R. L., Mastergeorge, A. M., & Coggins, T. E. (1983). The acquisition of communicative intentions in infants eight to fifteen months of age. *Language and Speech, 26*(2), 101-116.
Kaiser, A. P. (1993a). Functional language. In M. E. Snell (Ed.), *Instruction of students with severe disabilities: Fourth edition* (pp. 347-379). New York: Merrill.
Kaiser, A. P. (1993b). Parent-implemented language intervention: An environmental system perspective. In A. P. Kaiser & D. B. Gray (Eds.), *Enhancing children's communication: Research foundations for intervention* (Vol. 2) (pp. 63-84). Baltimore: Paul H. Brookes.

Kaiser, A. P., Yoder, P. J., & Keetz, A. (1992). Evaluating milieu teaching. In S. F. Warren & J. Reichle (Eds.), *Causes and effects in communication and language intervention: Volume 1* (pp. 9-47). Baltimore: Paul H. Brookes.

Linder, T. W. (1993). *Transdisciplinary play-based intervention: Guidelines for developing a meaningful curriculum for young children* (pp. 11-15). Baltimore: Paul H. Brookes.

McCathren, R. B. (2000). Teacher-implemented prelinguistic communication intervention. *Focus on Autism and Other Developmental Disabilities, 15*(1), 21-29.

McCathren, R. B., Yoder, P. J., & Warren, S. F. (1995). The role of directives in early intervention. *Journal of Early Intervention, 19*(2), 91-101.

McCathren, R. B., Yoder, P. J., & Warren, S. F. (1999). Prelinguistic pragmatic functions as predictors of later expressive vocabulary. *Journal of Early Intervention, 22*(3), 205-216.

Mundy, P., Kasari, C., Sigman, M., & Ruskin, E. (1995). Nonverbal communication and early language acquisition in children with Down syndrome and in normally developing children. *Journal of Speech and Hearing Research, 38*, 157-167.

Mundy, P., Sigman, M., & Kasari, C. (1990). A longitudinal study of joint attention and language development in autistic children. *Journal of Autism and Developmental Disorders, 20*(1), 115-128.

Ostrosky, M. M., & Kaiser, A. P. (1991). Preschool environments that promote communication. *Teaching Exceptional Children, 23*(4), 6-10.

Smith, L., & vonTetzchner, S. (1986). Communicative, sensorimotor, and language skills of young children with Down syndrome. *American Journal of Mental Deficiency, 91*(1), 57-66.

Stoel-Gammon, C. (1998). Role of babbling and phonology in early linguistic development. In A. Wetherby, S. F. Warren, & J. Reichle (Eds.), *Transitions in prelinguistic communication: Volume 7* (pp. 87-110). Baltimore: Paul H. Brookes.

Warren, S. F., & Yoder, P. J. (1998). Facilitating the transition from preintentional to intentional communication. In A. Wetherby, S. F. Warren, & J. Reichle (Eds.), *Transitions in prelinguistic communication: Volume 7* (pp. 365-384). Baltimore: Paul H. Brookes.

Warren, S. F., Yoder, P. J., Gazdag, G. E., Kim, K., & Jones, H. A. (1993). Facilitating prelinguistic communication skills in young children with developmental delay. *Journal of Speech and Hearing Research, 36*, 83-97.

Wetherby, A. M., Cain, D. H., Yonclas, D. G., & Walker, V. G. (1988). Analysis of intentional communication of normal children from the prelinguistic to the multiword stage. *Journal of Speech and Hearing Research, 31*, 240-252.

Wetherby, A. M., Warren, S. F., & Reichle, J. (1998). Introduction to transitions in prelinguistic communication. In A. Wetherby, S. F. Warren, & J. Reichle (Eds.), *Transitions in prelinguistic communication: Volume 7* (pp. 1-11). Baltimore: Paul H. Brookes.

Wilcox, M. J. (1992). Enhancing initial communication skills in young children with developmental disabilities through partner programming. *Seminars in Speech and Hearing, 13*, 194-212.

Yoder, P. J., & Warren, S. F. (1999). Maternal responsivity mediates the relationship between prelinguistic intentional communication and later language. *Journal of Early Intervention, 22*, 126-136.

Five Tools for Teaching Vocabulary in the Preschool Classroom

Laura Segebart DeThorne, M.A., University of Illinois at Urbana-Champaign
Ruth V. Watkins, Ph.D., University of Illinois at Urbana-Champaign

Inspired by the season's particularly large accumulation of snow, the current theme in Ms. Jameson's preschool classroom is "Winter Wonderland." It takes a few extra minutes to unwrap the children from their woolen layers before gathering around the rug for circle time.

"Good morning class. I'm so glad you *bundled up* today (Ms. Jameson wraps her arms around herself and shivers). There's even more snow than yesterday."

One mention of the snow and Danisha can hardly contain herself. "Ms. Jameson! Ms. Jameson! Him throwed a snowball at me!" Danisha exclaims and points to Daniel.

"He threw a snowball at you? That's another good reason to bundle up—extra padding."

Ms. Jameson continues, "I bundled up in my warmest coat and my fuzziest mittens. What did you bundle up in this morning?"

Several of the children answer at once.

Ms. Jameson summarizes, "You bundled up in coats and mittens and scarves and boots. Look Danisha, your boots are just like Avery's. They are *identical*—just the same. Both of you have purple boots with pink laces."

"Do you know what boots are good for?" Ms. Jameson continues. "They keep our feet warm when we *trudge* through the snow. I think that would be good for our morning exercise. Let's stand up and pretend we are all bundled up and trudging through the snow."

Ms. Jameson stands up, wraps her arms around herself, hunches up her shoulders as if fending off a fierce wind, and lifts her feet up and down laboriously.

The children follow suit, each in his or her own charmingly unique pantomime.

Introduction

For many children, vocabulary development is one of the most noticeable and exciting hallmarks of the preschool years. Infants typically progress from nonspecific, albeit persuasive, forms of nonverbal communication such as crying, to their first word, in approximately ten to 15 months. During their second year of life, children begin accumulating an estimated eight new words per day, a period often referred to as the vocabulary "spurt" (Dromi, 1999). By the time children enter school, most have accumulated a vocabulary of approximately 13,000 words, a repertoire that balloons to 60,000 by high school graduation (Pinker, 1999). What makes this vocabulary explosion all the more impressive is that, unlike reading or arithmetic, it is not explicitly taught—at least not initially.

Children are generally quite skilled at learning new vocabulary through simply hearing words during typical daily events and routines. Yet, word learning does not occur so effortlessly for all children. Some children have considerable difficulty with this area of language learning. Difficulty learning vocabulary often accompanies developmental disabilities such as Down syndrome and autism, but may also be apparent in children with relatively isolated language difficulties. Some children have difficulty learning vocabulary without any clear cause. In addition to children with language learning difficulties, children from backgrounds of poverty appear at risk for slowed rates of word learning. A number of recent investigations (Hart & Risley, 1995; Purcell-Gates, 1995) have revealed that children from low income families understand and use fewer different words than their middle income peers.

Regardless of the source, limited vocabulary skills make it more difficult for children to express their needs and ideas and place them at risk in key areas of development such as peer relations and reading achievement (Dickinson & Tabors, 2001; Gertner, Rice, & Hadley, 1994; Lombardino, Riccio, Hynd, & Pinheiro, 1997). For example, Gertner and colleagues (1994) reported that children who scored higher on a standardized test of vocabulary comprehension were more apt to be identified as "liked" by their peers. In addition, a recent longitudinal project by Snow and her colleagues (as cited in Dickinson & Tabors, 2001) revealed that vocabulary knowledge is a strong predictor of early reading outcomes. For these reasons, promoting vocabulary development is an important goal for all preschool children.

Perhaps more than other areas of language (e.g., grammar), vocabulary development appears significantly influenced by the quantity and quality of language input children receive. Consequently, teachers, parents, and peers play an important role in facilitating a child's vocabulary growth. As exemplified in the introductory vignette, this article focuses on the preschool environment and provides five general strategies, or "tools," that can be used by regular and special early childhood teachers and staff to facilitate children's vocabulary development (see Table 1). These strategies are based on three premises that are consistent with DEC recommended practices (Sandall, McLean, & Smith, 2000): (1) teachers have the ability to exert a significant influence on children's vocabulary development; (2) children learn best in a naturalistic setting that values communication and facilitates meaningful interaction—not only between teacher and child but between children as well; and (3) vocabulary development is an important skill for preschool children not only because it affects their ability to express their wants and needs, but also because it is linked to social development and later literacy achievement.

Table 1: Five Tools for Teaching Vocabulary in the Classroom

T	Talk a lot and encourage talking.
O	Offer sophisticated words.
O	Overdo it with repetition.
L	Leave contextual clues.
S	Stress new words.

The five strategies recommended are derived from solid research based on typically developing children, children with language disabilities, and children considered "at risk" for school failure. The strategies are very general and are intended to benefit all preschool children regardless of developmental level or disability type. Despite their broad applicability, these strategies have not been explicitly researched across all disability types. Differences in learning styles may require that some strategies be adapted for individual children. In addition, these teaching strategies are not meant to replace the individualized assistance that children with language disabilities receive from speech-language pathologists and other specialized professionals.

Talk a Lot and Encourage Talking

Perhaps the most straightforward and intuitive tool for teaching vocabulary development in the classroom is to increase the use of words by developing an environment that values communication. More words, produced by teachers and children alike, increases the number of word learning opportunities. Studies have found strong positive correlations between the number of words children hear, both at home and at preschool, and the size of their vocabularies (Dickinson, Cote, & Smith, 1993; Hart & Risley, 1995; Huttenlocher, Haight, Bryk, Seltzer, & Lyons, 1991).

Certainly the burden of talking should not fall solely on the teacher. In addition to listening, children need to be given the chance to use words in fun and meaningful conversations. Children are often highly motivated to learn the vocabulary of their peers. Consequently, providing opportunities for children to use words in the classroom gives them the chance to learn from each other. The following example demonstrates how a teacher might arrange the environment to encourage children to talk with one another.

The dramatic play center in Ms. Jameson's class changes each week according to the theme. This week the center contains a box full of hats, gloves, coats, boots, and scarves. In addition, there are a couple child-sized shovels and a box full of packing peanuts so the children can pretend to scoop snow.

Adam picks up a shovel.

"Adam, bundle up!" Danisha scolds with a maternal tone.

"Up?" Adam replies.

"Yes, here's a hat and gloves ... and a coat," Danisha labels each item for him as she takes them out of the box.

Offer Sophisticated Words

Although an increased amount of talking in general appears to facilitate vocabulary development, the sophistication of the words used also appears to be an important variable. Sophisticated, in this context, refers to words that are unfamiliar to most preschoolers, words like *trudge* and *identical* as used in the introductory vignette. A longitudinal study of the home and school factors that support literacy development in low income children between the ages of three and nine found that exposing preschool children to new and "sophisticated" words is a particularly important tool for broadening their vocabularies (Beals, 1997; Beals & Tabors, 1995; Weizman & Snow, in press). Of particular relevance, a study by Dickinson, Cote, and Smith (1993) found that the more sophisticated words children heard from their preschool teachers, the larger the number of words they were likely to understand as kindergartners.

If, as it appears, children's vocabulary size is affected by the number and sophistication of words heard, then increasing word use and paying particular attention to modeling rich, novel vocabulary in the classroom will be beneficial. Words can be used to provide labels not only for concrete objects and attributes, but also for less tangible constructs such as actions (e.g., trudging), feelings (e.g., surprised), and categories (e.g., seasons, colors, fruit). In general, most teachers are skilled at modeling basic vocabulary, such as object labels, colors, and shapes. Remembering to use some novel and sophisticated words may be more difficult. The following vignette highlights the use of words to label actions during gym class and includes a couple of more sophisticated verbs, such as *kneel* and *hurl*.

The students in Ms. Jameson's class have bundled up and gathered outside for gym class.

"Let's find some fresh snow," the gym teacher states. "We're going to play Simon Says. Here we go!"

"Simon says, *kneel* in the snow." The gym teacher gets down on one knee and most of the children kneel accordingly.

"Simon says, lay down in the snow on your back."

"Simon says, move your arms up and down."

"Simon says, move your feet side to side."

"You've made a snow angel!"

"Simon says, stand up and make a snowball."

"Simon says, *hurl* the snowball toward the tree."

"Now, make another snowball."

"Gotcha!"

Overdo it With Repetition

Not only is it beneficial for children to hear lots of words and more challenging vocabulary, but it's also helpful for them to hear these new words over and over again—particularly in meaningful contexts. Though children may be able to derive some sense of a word's meaning after hearing it used only once, hearing the word used additional times, particularly across different contexts, helps specify and solidify its meaning. There is some evidence to suggest that when new words are repeated as many as ten times in a single day, children with language learning difficulties are able to learn as many new words as their typically developing peers (Rice, Oetting, Marquis, Bode, & Pae, 1994). Though ten repetitions might sound impractical for a classroom setting, consider how many times the word *bundle* is used in the introductory vignette: six times. In addition, other opportunities would likely present themselves throughout the course of the day, particularly if the day's activities were built around a theme, such as "Winter Wonderland."

There are no clear guidelines regarding how many times new words should be repeated. The number depends on many variables, such as the abstractness of the word, each child's word learning capabilities, and the presence of meaningful opportunities. However, what is clear is that repeating new words across a variety of contexts facilitates word learning (Wilcox, Kouri, & Caswell, 1991). The following example extends the word *identical*, as used in the introductory vignette, to a different classroom activity and models its use four more times.

The children are carefully cutting paper snowflakes for their art activity. After they finish, the teacher lays them all out on the table for comparison.

"Remember what we read about snowflakes in our book? What did we learn about snowflakes, Adam?" Ms. Jameson prompts.

"We eat 'em!" Danisha shouts.

"I'm asking Adam," Ms. Jameson reiterates.

"Eat," Adam offers.

"That's right," Ms. Jameson smiles and nods, "You can eat them. We also learned that no two snowflakes are *identical*. No two are the same. They're all different."

"How are Danisha's and Adam's snowflakes different?" Ms. Jameson prompts.

"Him is big," Daniel asserts.

"You're right. Adam's snowflake is bigger than Danisha's. They are not *identical*. No two snowflakes are *identical*. Just like none of us are *identical*."

Leave Contextual Clues

Certainly repetition itself does not ensure word learning. If it did, we would learn words much like we do multiplication tables. Instead, new words are best learned when embedded in an informative context full of clues to word meaning (Beals, 1997; Dickinson & Tabors, 1991; Weizman & Snow, in press). Informative contexts can take at least two forms: the environmental context that children see and the spoken context that they hear. The environmental context often includes the object or action to which the new word refers. For example, during art a teacher might tell a child to stop *twirling* the scissors or might refer to a child's paper snowflake as looking like *lace*. Speaking of what children are focused upon at any particular moment helps them associate new words with the actions and objects in their surroundings. Evidence suggests that word learning is particularly likely within informal activities such as free-play and mealtime, perhaps in part because the adult is more apt to focus on the child's interests during these times (Beals, 1997; Beals & Tabors, 1995; Dickinson, Cote, & Smith, 1993).

Regardless of the activity, the discourse surrounding new words can provide information, either directly or indirectly, regarding word meaning. For example, in the introductory vignette, Ms. Jameson provides indirect information regarding the meaning of *bundled up* by including it within a discussion of winter and coats and mittens, etc. She provides direct information regarding the word *identical* when she states that it means *"just the same."* The following vignette exemplifies how a child might use clues from the environmental context regarding a word's meaning (i.e., being in music class, playing instruments, etc.) as well as how a teacher might provide direct information regarding a word's meaning.

The children sit in a loose circle during music class, each with a pair of wooden sticks and an upside down plastic basin. The lyrics "I like to play the drum ..." float into the hallway as each child hammers out an individual rhythm.

The music teacher holds up a card with a lower case "f" written in italics, and Daniel begins banging his drum loudly.

"That's right, Daniel. The 'f' stands for 'forte' and that means 'loud.'"

The teacher takes up the melody and the beat as she continues her song, "I like to play the drum ... play a little louder ...."

The children need little encouragement as they increase their volume.

Stress New Words

Although the discourse surrounding new words can provide clues to meaning, it potentially could cause the new word to "get lost" amidst a seemingly continuous stream of speech. It is difficult for new language learners to determine where one word ends and the next one begins. Consequently, stressing new words or using them in a way that makes them more noticeable facilitates word learning (Bedore & Leonard, 1995; Weismer, 1997; Weismer & Hesketh, 1998). Examples of how to make a new word more noticeable include altering a word's loudness or pitch (e.g., "He rode the *toboggan* down the slope."); preceding the new word by a slight pause (e.g., "He rode the ... toboggan down the slope."); or using the new word in sentence-final position (e.g., "This is a toboggan.").

In addition to how words are spoken, visual cues such as objects, gestures, and facial expressions help stress or call attention to new words. For example, if a teacher were introducing the word "toboggan," having a picture or having an actual toboggan for the children to touch and ride would make the word even more memorable. Consequently, books, movies, and field trips can provide visual cues for new words of interest to children that are not typically encountered in the classroom (e.g., mountain, skiing, sled). Though more abstract than objects, facial expression and gestures can also provide visual cues to make a word more noticeable and help children understand its meaning (Fazio, 2001). For example, raising one's eyebrows in excitement when referring to a toboggan not only calls children's attention to the word but also helps build the children's concept of the word as a fun plaything. Gestures can serve a similar function, for example, making a sliding motion with one's hand when referring to the word "toboggan." The following example highlights a teacher's use of both ges-tural and spoken emphasis on the everyday words *hat* and *coat*.

As the children begin preparing to go home at the end of the school day, Kevin mutters, "That's all folks! That's all folks!" and circles around the room with a flurry of energy.

Ms. Jameson guides him over to his cubby and replies, "That's right, Kevin. It's time to go home."

She touches the top of her head and says, "Let's put on your *hat*." She puts on his hat.

Ms. Jameson then folds her arms over her chest and states "Let's put on your *coat*." She grabs his parka from the cubby and guides his arms through the sleeves.

Conclusion

Because many preschool curricula offer specific guidelines regarding what vocabulary to teach, this article has focused on *how* to promote vocabulary in the classroom and suggests only that the words be func-tional, relevant, interesting, and, to a certain degree, challenging. Five general strategies, or "tools," for promoting such vocabulary were described and exemplified: (1) talk a lot and encourage talking, (2) offer sophisticated words, (3) overdo it with word repetition, (4) leave con-textual clues, and (5) stress new words. Though the specific examples may vary, these same tools are useful in promoting vocabulary develop-ment across settings and can also be used by parents, daycare providers, and a variety of therapists. One of the most encouraging aspects of vocabulary development is that it is substantially influenced by environ-mental input. Consequently, parents and teachers can have a positive influence on children's vocabulary development, and in doing so can increase the likelihood of children's social and academic success.

Notes

You can reach Laura Segebart DeThorne by e-mail at lauras@uiuc.edu

Preparation of this manuscript was supported in part by training grant #H029D60035 from the U.S. Department of Education, Office of Special Education Programs; Jim Halle, PI; Ruth Watkins, Michaelene Ostrosky, and Cynthia Johnson, Co-PIs.

References

Beals, D. (1997). Sources of support for learning words in conversation: Evidence from mealtimes. *Journal of Child Language*, 24(3), 673-684.

Beals, D., & Tabors, P. (1995). Arboretum, bureaucratic, and carbohydrates. *Applied Psycholinguistics*, 14(4), 489-513.

Bedore, L. M., & Leonard, L. B. (1995). Prosodic and syntactic bootstrapping and their clinical applica-tions: A tutorial. *American Journal of Speech-Language Pathology*, 4(1), 66-72.

Dickinson, D. K., Cote, L. R., & Smith, M. W. (1993). Learning vocabulary in preschool: Social and discourse contexts affecting vocabulary growth. In W. Damon & C. Daiute (Eds.), *New directions in child development (Vol. 61): The development of literacy through social interaction* (pp. 68-78). San Francisco: Jossey-Bass.

Dickinson, D. K., & Tabors, P. O. (1991). Early literacy: Linkages between home, school, and literacy achievement at age five. *Journal of Research in Childhood Education, 6*(1), 30-46.

Dickinson, D. K., & Tabors, P. O. (Eds.). (2001). *Beginning literacy with language: Young children learning at home and school*. Baltimore: Paul H. Brookes.

Dromi, E. (1999). Early lexical development. In M. Barrett (Ed.), *The development of language* (pp. 99-126). East Sussex, UK: Psychology Press Ltd.

Fazio, B. B. (2001, June 6). *Do iconic gestures facilitate novel word learning in preschool children with and without SLI?* Poster presented at the annual Symposium on Research in Child Language Disorders, Madison, WI.

Gertner, B., Rice, M. L., & Hadley, P. A. (1994). Influence of communicative competence on peer preferences in a preschool classroom. *Journal of Speech and Hearing Research, 37*(4), 913-923.

Hart, B., & Risley, T. R. (1995). *Meaningful differences in the everyday experience of young American children*. Baltimore: Paul H. Brookes.

Huttenlocher, J., Haight, W., Bryk, A., Seltzer, M., & Lyons, T. (1991). Early vocabulary growth: Relation to language input and gender. *Developmental Psychology, 27*(2), 236-248.

Lombardino, L. J., Riccio, C. A., Hynd, G. W., & Pinheiro, S. B. (1997). Linguistic deficits in children with reading disabilities. *American Journal of Speech Language Pathology, 6*(3), 71-78.

Pinker, S. (1999). *Words and rules: The ingredients of language*. New York: Basic Books.

Purcell-Gates, V. (1995). *Other people's words: The cycle of low literacy*. Cambridge, MA: Harvard University Press.

Rice, M. L., Oetting, J. B., Marquis, J., Bode, J., & Pae, S. (1994). Frequency of input effects on word comprehension of children with specific language impairment. *Journal of Speech and Hearing Research, 37*(1), 106-122.

Sandall, S., McLean, M. E., & Smith, B. J. (2000). *DEC recommended practices in early intervention/early childhood special education*. Longmont, CO: Sopris West.

Weismer, S. E. (1997). The role of stress in language processing and intervention. *Topics in Language Disorders, 17*(4), 41-52.

Weismer, S. E., & Hesketh, L. J. (1998). The impact of emphatic stress on novel word learning by children with specific language impairment. *Journal of Speech, Language, and Hearing Research, 41*(6), 1444-1458.

Weizman, Z. O., & Snow, C. E. (in press). Lexical input as related to children's vocabulary acquisition: Effects of sophisticated exposure and support for meaning. *Developmental Psychology*.

Wilcox, J. M., Kouri, T., & Caswell, S. B. (1991). Early language intervention: A comparison of classroom and individual treatment. *American Journal of Speech-Language Pathology, 1*(1), 49-62.

"Hey! I'm Talking to You": A Naturalistic Procedure to Teach Preschool Children to Use Their AAC Systems With Peers

Ann N. Garfinkle, Ph.D., Vanderbilt University
Ilene S. Schwartz, Ph.D., University of Washington

Chantal is a little girl who knows what she likes. These include figurines of people and animals, doll houses, pictures of her family, and any salty food. Since her teacher taught her to use an AAC system with computer-generated symbols, Chantal can ask adults for preferred items effectively and efficiently. Her teachers and parents are pleased with her new communication skills, but very concerned that she does not interact very often with peers.

Introduction

Chantal, diagnosed with global developmental disabilities, like many other children with disabilities who have significant delays in language and communication, uses an augmentative or adaptive communication (AAC) system. An AAC system consists of techniques and devices (both high and low tech) to either facilitate the intelligibility of a student's speech or enable a student to communicate without using speech. Some AAC systems such as simple sign language and communication books with symbols are found frequently in early childhood special education settings. Although many children with disabilities learn to use AAC systems effectively with adult communicative partners, they rarely use their AAC systems with other children. This lack of peer-directed communication interferes with children engaging in positive social interactions and developing meaningful social relationships with peers.

Social relationships are best developed through successful, repeated interactions with typically developing peers (Kennedy, Horner, &

Newton, 1989). Unfortunately, this experience often constitutes a major problem for children with special needs (McCormick & Schiefelbusch, 1990) and is further complicated when children with special needs use an AAC system as their primary form of communication (Carter & Maxwell, 1998).

For children who use AAC systems as their primary functional mode of communication, having the AAC system present is not sufficient to ensure that peer interactions will take place (Warrick, 1988). There are many barriers that explain this phenomenon, including: AAC systems may be an unfamiliar mode of communication for peers; AAC systems sometimes result in slower message transmission than speech (Beukelman & Mirenda, 1992); the users of AAC systems tend to use their systems infrequently (Calculator & Dollaghan, 1982; Harris, 1982; Houghton, Bronicki, & Guess, 1987); and children who use AAC systems tend to spend the majority of their conversational time as responders rather then initiators of interactions (Yoder & Kraat, 1983).

Despite the importance of social development and the barriers for children who use AAC systems to develop these skills, relatively few studies have examined the effects of peer training on the social communication of children who use AAC systems (Carter & Maxwell, 1998). The studies that have been conducted (Light & Collier, 1986; McNaughton & Light, 1989) suggest that interventions should focus on developing communication skills of the individuals who use an AAC system and also the partners with whom they communicate.

The following intervention was designed to teach preschool-age children to use their AAC systems with their classroom peers. The intervention was empirically validated to increase social interactions in training and in generalization settings in integrated preschool classrooms (Garfinkle & Schwartz, 1994; Schwartz, Garfinkle, & Bauer, 1998). This naturalistic intervention strategy was designed to be implemented during regularly occurring small group times and to provide opportunities for children who use AAC systems to initiate social interaction as well as respond to peers' initiations. Although the intervention was designed specifically for use with the Picture Exchange Communication System (PECS) (Frost & Bondy, 1992), it is compatible for use with a wide variety of both high and low tech AAC systems. The intervention, which is outlined in Table 1, uses the teaching and environmental support procedures described in the DEC recommended practices (Sandall, McLean, & Smith, 2000).

Table 1: Using AAC for Peer Interactions: The Intervention in Four Steps

Step 1:	Make sure that the target child is a fluent and persistent user of the AAC system.
Step 2:	Arrange the small group environment so that children are responsible for distributing the materials needed to participate in the small group activity.
	Step 2a: Make sure peers have materials that are preferred by the target child.
	Step 2b: Make sure the target child has materials needed to participate in the small group activity, but not his or her preferred materials.
Step 3:	Support (through prompting) successful peer-to-peer social interactions.
Step 4:	Make sure that the peer interaction skills generalize across peers, materials, and environments.

Foundational Conditions

In order for this intervention to be successful, the following five conditions are important to have in place prior to the start of the peer interaction intervention: (1) fluent use of the AAC system with adults; (2) persistence in using the system to communicate desires, wants, and needs; (3) a system that is easily understood by people with no additional or little formal training in understanding the system; (4) a system which is efficient; and (5) a system which is effective.

Fluent Use of System With Adults

In order to most efficiently teach a child to use an AAC system with a peer, the target child should be able to fluently use the system with adults who are generally more competent and more consistent communicative partners than are preschool-age children.

Persistence

As previously stated, adults are more consistent and competent communicators than are preschoolers. It can be assumed that not all of the initiations toward peers made by children who use AAC systems will be successful. Thus, the child who uses the AAC system should be taught to persist in the use of the system in order to deliver the message. The Picture Exchange Communication System (PECS) (Frost & Bondy, 1992) has an entire phase of the training devoted to teaching persistence. In this part of the training the communicative partner (i.e., adult) systematically moves away from the child, turns away from the child, and ignores initial attempts at communication. In our experience, this step of the training is essential in teaching robust communication skills that can be used with less willing or competent communicative partners (e.g., peers). Training of other AAC systems may not include this step.

For users of such systems, spending some time to develop persistence skills may make the peer intervention more efficient.

Easily Understood System

When preschool-age children are communicating with peers, even typically developing communicative partners will still be learning communications skills. Thus the form in which the message is delivered is important and should be as intuitive as possible. By using a form of communication that requires extensive training to understand, the number of potential communicative partners is greatly reduced.

An Efficient System

Speech is an efficient form of communication because it happens quickly. AAC systems must also be efficient. If it takes too long to communicate, the moment may be gone. Further, if there are other behaviors that are more efficient (e.g., grabbing), then it is likely that the child who uses the AAC system is going to use the most efficient means to deliver the message.

An Effective System

The AAC system must be effective. In other words, the target child should be able to learn to use the system quickly, and the system should be flexible enough so that the user can communicate his or her message efficiently.

Environmental Arrangement

If the foundational conditions described are in place, then the child who uses the AAC system is ready to begin regular, supported, systematic practice in interacting with peers. The first step in the intervention is to arrange an environment that: (1) establishes classroom rules that support

respect, reciprocity, and sharing; (2) ensures the availability of both personal and class-wide AAC systems; (3) embeds predictable and structured practice into daily activities; (4) provides access to consistent, multiple peer partners; and (5) selects and distributes materials to promote peer interactions.

Rules That Support Reciprocity

In order for the child who uses an AAC system to have successful, adequate practice in reciprocal communicative exchanges with classroom peers, clear expectations for these interactions must be communicated by the teacher to the children. This is most easily accomplished with a combination of simple, explicit rules announced by the teacher (e.g., "In this class we share"); teacher support of sharing (e.g., prompts that facilitate sharing); and teacher praise of sharing (e.g., "Jim and Bob shared the car!"). These rules and supports create an atmosphere of respect, reciprocity, and sharing that is necessary to facilitate successful social interactions between the target child and his or her peers.

System Availability

A child must have access to the ACC system throughout the day. Further, access to the system and use of the system must be quick. Each child who uses an ACC system needs his or her own system, which they have ready access to and are taught to be responsible for (i.e., are taught to bring the system to snack, small group, and other class activities). Depending on the AAC system, it may be helpful to also have class-wide systems available for the use of children in the class. Free-play centers, outside playgrounds, and gyms may be environments in which class-wide centers are more efficient than individual systems.

Predictable and Structured Practice

In order for children who use AAC systems to be able to learn to use the system with peers, there must be daily predictable and structured practice. This practice is most easily accomplished during a small group time. The peer interaction practice is then embedded into the activity that has been planned for small group.

Consistent, Multiple Peer Partners

The small group should consist of three to five children. These children should remain consistent over time. This consistency gives both the AAC user and the peer(s) an opportunity to learn, over time, how to communicate with each other. This familiarity also facilitates friendships that may transfer to other activities during the preschool day.

Selection and Distribution of Materials

Although the intervention will be embedded in the ongoing small group activity, some adaptations may need to be made. In order to increase the likelihood that the child who uses an AAC system will want to communicate with a peer, the peer should be in possession of something that the child who uses an AAC system wants. Thus it is important to plan activities, or augment materials, so that the preferences of the child who uses an AAC system have been considered. Instead of having the teacher pass out the small group materials, the children will do so, but only after their peers have asked them to do so. For example, if the small group activity is playing with modeling dough, one child may be in charge of passing out the dough; another would be in charge of cookie cutters (including the letter cookie cutters which are the favorite of the child using the AAC system); another might have rolling pins; another knives; and another garlic presses. This way all the children, including the target child, have the responsibility of asking for what they want and responding to peers who ask for needed materials.

On subsequent days preferred materials should be rotated among all the children in the small group so that the children have practice communicating with multiple peers. Also, make sure that the child who uses an AAC system also has materials. This ensures that the peers will make initiations toward the child who uses the AAC system. In other words, the teacher should engineer the material selection and placement so that there is a high likelihood that the children will need to interact with each other in order to obtain the materials they want to participate in the small group activity.

Teacher Supports

The role of the teacher in this intervention is very important and yet also very specific. In this intervention, the teacher engineers the environment in order to set the stage for the peer interaction to occur. The teacher's job, however, is also to provide support so that the peer-to-peer interaction is successful, yet not be a "conduit" through which information from the children passes.

Support for the Target Child

When initially teaching the child who uses an AAC system to communicate with peers using the AAC device, the teacher will need to provide prompts. A prompt is a form of instructional assistance that precedes the child's response, facilitates correct responding, and can be removed (i.e., faded) quickly to allow for independent child responding. The prompts should help the child who uses the AAC system to get the attention of the peer and to make a request for a material using the AAC system. A rate of one initiation per each minute and a half should help strike a balance between asking for preferred materials and actually using the materials to participate in the small group activity. The teacher may also need to support the child who uses the AAC system in responding to peer initiations. This can be done by helping the child who uses the AAC system attend to the initiations made by peers, and provide help to comply with peers' requests.

Support for Peers

Even if the AAC system is easily understandable, the teacher will initially need to assist the peers. This support should be provided incidentally but systematically. In other words, the teacher does not need to provide a class-wide inservice on responding to AAC systems. Rather, as the child who uses the AAC system initiates to a peer, the teacher can prompt the peer through a response. One efficient way to provide this peer support is to help the peer attend to the initiation, help the peer attend to the form of the communication, and help the peer respond appropriately to the initiation.

Chantal's teacher, Ruth, decides that it is time to teach Chantal to use her AAC system with peers. She decides to use the first small group activity of the day as her teaching time. For the first day of instruction Ruth decides to use the doll house and associated figurines. She gives Chantal the vehicles, Serena the people figurines, and Toby the animal figurines. Chantal asks Ruth for the people figurines, and Ruth replies, "I don't have them; ask Serena." Chantal asks Serena, and Ruth says, "Serena, what is Chantal saying?" Serena hands a figurine to Chantal. After prompting a few more interactions like this, Ruth steps back and watches the children interact.

Plans for Generalization

The vignette intervention takes place during small group time, within an environment designed to increase peer interactions and with teacher behavior designed to ensure that successful interactions occur. However, the child who uses the AAC system must be able to communicate with multiple peers, for multiple materials, and in multiple settings. There is empirical support that suggests that this intervention results in this type of generalized skill. This generalization is more than likely the result of the environmental arrangement described previously. Due to the importance of the generalization of skills, a description of planning for generalization across peers, materials, and environments is provided next.

Across Peers

In order for generalization across peers to occur, the intervention should be implemented with multiple peers. This is important so that the child who uses the AAC system learns that communication is possible with many peers, not just a select one or two peers.

Across Materials

As previously stated, the teacher may need to adapt the small group materials to include preferred items. While this is essential for creating an environment in which the child who uses an AAC device is likely to initiate to peers, it is equally as important to make sure that the child is interacting with peers around a number of different materials. For children who like many materials, this does not pose a problem. For children who have a limited repertoire, this is more problematic. It is recommended that the teacher continually encourage the target child to interact with many materials to determine which of these materials become preferred, and then to incorporate those materials into the small group time.

Across Environments

In order for the target child's skills to generalize to new environments, the new environment must support the child who uses the AAC system. This means that the child will need access to his or her AAC system across all activities in the classroom, at daycare, home, and in the community. Just as important, the child will need a context in which there is a reason to communicate. There must be materials in which the child who uses the AAC system is interested in multiple environments, and access to these materials must depend (at least some of the time) on peer interaction. In some cases, where the environment supports this type of interaction, the child will need some initial teacher support to have success using the system in the new environment.

Troubleshooting

Even with careful implementation of the intervention as described in this article, there are bound to be days when the intervention does not seem to be effective. When this happens, consult our "Troubleshooting Guide" (see Table 2). This guide is designed to provide solutions to the most common difficulties associated with this intervention.

Table 2: Troubleshooting Guide

Problem	Possible Cause(s)	Possible Solution(s)
Target Child's Behavior		
The target child is not initiating communication	The target child does not realize that the nature of the activity has changed so that in order to participate, he or she needs to initiate.	The target child may need to be prompted a couple of times in order to learn the demands of the new context.
The target child initiates communication, but directs the communication toward the adult	The target child has, in the past, only been successful communicating with adults and does not view peers as potential communicative partners.	Redirect the target child to the peer and support the interaction so that it is a successful peer-to-peer interaction.
The target child initiates communication toward a peer, but fails to get the peer's attention	The target child may not be persistent in his or her attempts to initiate toward peers.	The target child may need to be taught other attention-getting strategies, such as tapping the peer on the shoulder, looking at the peer, etc.
The target child initiates communication toward the peer and gains the peer's attention, but does not complete the communicative exchange	Because the process took too long, the target child has changed his or her mind.	Help the children complete the exchange, and, in future exchanges, provide support so that the communication is efficient.
	The target child does not really want the requested item, but rather wants the peer's attention.	Provide alternative ways for the target child to get the peer's attention. These can include teaching greetings (e.g., "Hi" or a "high five") or play entry strategies (i.e., peer initiation).
	The target child did not really want the requested item, but instead wanted a different item.	Help the peer complete the exchange for the requested item and provide support to the target child to make a new request for the desired item.

continued

Problem	Possible Cause(s)	Possible Solution(s)
Peer's Behavior		
Peer does not acknowledge the target child's initiation	The peer does not realize that the target child's communication is directed at him or her.	Narrate for the peer the target child's communicative behavior and prompt appropriate responses.
	The peer does not understand the target child's initiation.	Provide instruction so that the peer understands the communicative function of the AAC system.
Peer does not understand the target child's request	The form of the AAC system is new to the peer.	Teach the peer how the AAC system works and how it communicates.
	The form of the AAC system is poorly articulated.	Make sure that the AAC system itself is in good working order.
Peer makes an initiation to the target child, but does not get the target child's attention	The target child did not notice the peer initiation.	Teach the peer to use a variety of strategies to gain the target child's attention, such as calling the child's name, using gestures, etc.
	The target child did not understand the peer initiation.	Provide prompting so that the target child can engage in the interaction.
Peer makes an initiation but overanticipates the target child's response by taking the requested object	This peer hasn't had experience successfully communicating with the target child.	Provide support so that there is a successful peer-to-peer interaction.
	The target child is taking too long to respond.	Provide support so that there is a successful peer-to-peer interaction.

Conclusion

When this intervention is implemented and difficulties with the implementation of the intervention are addressed using the "Troubleshooting Guide," preschool-age children with a range of different diagnoses can learn to use their AAC systems effectively with their classroom peers. In our experience with this intervention, once children begin to communicate with their peers during structured times such as small group, interactions during less structured times such as recess and free choice are also observed. Also, we have observed a wide variety of interactions increasing, not just interactions using the AAC system. In other words, by teaching this communication skill one facilitates changes in social interaction and the complexity of children's play. Interventions such as this should become commonplace in early childhood educational settings. For it is only through the successful experience of social interaction that children with and without disabilities will learn the skills necessary to interact socially and grow developmentally.

Note
You can reach Ann N. Garfinkle by e-mail at ann.garfinkle@vanderbilt.edu

References

Beukelman, D. R., & Mirenda, P. (1992). *Augmentative and alternative communication: Management of severe communication disorders in children and adults.* Baltimore: Paul H. Brookes.

Calculator, S., & Dollaghan, C. (1982). The use of communication boards in a residential setting: An evaluation. *Journal of Speech and Hearing Disorders, 47*(3), 281-287.

Carter, M., & Maxwell, K. (1998). Promoting interaction with children using augmentative communication through a peer-directed intervention. *International Journal of Disabilities, Development, and Education, 45*(1), 75-96.

Frost, L., & Bondy, A. (1992). *PECS: The Picture Exchange Communication System training manual.* Cherry Hill, NJ: Pyramid Educational Consultants.

Garfinkle, A. N., & Schwartz, I. S. (1994, November 18). *PECS with peers: Increasing social interaction in an integrated preschool.* Paper presented at the annual convention for the Association for the Severely Handicapped, San Francisco, CA.

Harris, D. (1982). Communicative interaction processes involving nonvocal physically handicapped children. *Topics in Language Disorders, 2*(2), 21-37.

Houghton, J., Bronicki, G. J. B., & Guess, D. (1987). Opportunities to express preferences and make choices among students with severe disabilities in classroom settings. *Journal of the Association for Persons With Severe Handicaps, 12*(1), 18-27.

Kennedy, C. H., Horner, R. H., & Newton, J. S. (1989). Social contacts of adults with severe disabilities living in the community: A descriptive analysis of relationship patterns. *Journal of the Association for Persons With Severe Handicaps, 14*(2), 190-196.

Light, J., & Collier, B. (1986). Facilitating the development of effective initiation strategies by nonspeaking, physically disabled children. In S. W. Blackston (Ed.), *Augmentative communication: An introduction* (pp. 369-375). Rockville, MD: American Speech-Language and Hearing Association.

McCormick, L., & Schiefelbusch, R. L. (1990). *Early language intervention: An introduction.* Columbus, OH: Merrill.

McNaughton, D., & Light, J. (1989). Teaching facilitators to support the communication skills of an adult with severe cognitive disabilities: A case study. *Augmentative and Alternative Communication, 5*(1), 35-41.

Sandall, S., McLean, M. E., & Smith, B. J. (2000). *DEC recommended practices in early intervention/early childhood special education.* Longmont, CO: Sopris West.

Schwartz, I. S., Garfinkle, A. N., & Bauer, J. (1998). The Picture Exchange Communication System: Communication outcomes for young children with disabilities. *Topics in Early Childhood Special Education, 18*(3), 144-159.

Yoder, D., & Kraat, A. (1983). Intervention issues in nonspeech communication. In J. Miller, D. Yoder, & R. L. Schiefelbusch (Eds.), *Contemporary issues in nonspeech communication: ASHA reports* (pp. 27-51). Rockville, MD: American Speech-Language and Hearing Association.

Warrick, A. (1988). Sociocommunicative considerations within augmentative and alternative communication. *Augmentative and Alternative Communication, 4*(1), 45-51.

Embedded Learning Opportunities as an Instructional Strategy for Supporting Children's Learning in Inclusive Programs

Eva Horn, Ph.D., University of Kansas
Joan Lieber, Ph.D., University of Maryland
Susan Sandall, Ph.D., University of Washington
Ilene Schwartz, Ph.D., University of Washington

Jared is an only child who stayed at home with his mother until his third birthday, when he began attending a preschool. McAllister Child Care is an urban program primarily serving the employees of the downtown businesses. The program has never included a child with Down syndrome. Yet, the staff prides themselves in supporting all children's learning. They are eager to appropriately support Jared and his family as members of their program. Jared, however, has arrived with an IEP with goals that must be addressed. His preschool teacher remarks, "But I don't have time to do any one-to-one instruction with him."

A Rationale for Embedding Instruction

Concerns such as these are real for many early childhood providers. A primary difference between early childhood education (ECE) and early childhood special education (ECSE) is typically the degree to which individualized programs are implemented for children (Wolery & Wilbers, 1994). Although most early childhood environments offer learning opportunities across the day, children with disabilities may need guidance and support in order to recognize and learn from these opportunities. To address this, many professionals have recommended embedding instruction into existing classroom activities and routines (e.g., Bricker

& Cripe, 1992; Davis, Kilgo, & Gamel-McCormick, 1998; Noonan & McCormick, 1995; Wolery & Wilbers, 1994). Embedding is defined as " ... a procedure in which children are given opportunities to practice individual goals and objectives that are included within an activity or event in a manner that expands, modifies, or adapts the activity/event while remaining meaningful and interesting to children" (Bricker, Pretti-Frontczak, & McComas, 1998, p. 13).

Drawing on previous research around the instructional use of embedding (e.g., Fox & Hanline, 1993; Mudd & Wolery, 1987; Peck, Killen, & Baumgart, 1989; Venn et al., 1993; Venn & Wolery, 1992) and the developmental work by Bricker and colleagues (Bricker et al., 1998) related to activity-based interventions, we designed an instructional strategy termed embedded learning opportunities (ELO) (Horn, Lieber, Sandall, Schwartz, & Li, 2000; Sandall et al., in press). ELO is based on the premise that for many child objectives or goals providing access to the general early childhood curriculum is insufficient. We need to provide instruction through modeling, verbal prompting, and physical guidance in order for children with special needs to learn new or more complex skills within the context of the general curriculum and preschool environment. Teachers should identify the opportunities that are most salient to individualized learning objectives and embed short, systematic instructional interactions that support children's achievement of goals within existing routines and activities. For example, rather than setting up special sessions for teaching "object labels," the learning task is embedded into the ongoing activities: naming body parts might be embedded during doll play, naming items of clothing could be embedded in gross motor games such as Simon Says, and labeling foods and eating utensils could be embedded in lunch or lunch preparation. Further, if a "refined grasp" is a child's learning objective, instruction could be provided by embedding the use of this grasp during snack with a raisin, apple slice, or cheese wedge, or during an art activity that includes picking up pieces of tape.

With ELO the activities and routines become the structure for supporting children's learning. Many of the activities are child-initiated, so we know they are motivating (Bricker & Cripe, 1992). By embedding effective instruction into fun and motivating activities learning often occurs more quickly (Losardo & Bricker, 1994). More important, since the children have learned the skill in a more natural setting they are able to use the skill when they need it to obtain an item or participate in an activity. Table 1 illustrates the concepts of use of skills in natural settings; across contexts, materials, and activities; and with different people.

Table 1: Illustration of ELO Implementation

Context	Scenario
Natural Routine	Jared's juice glass is empty. He signs "more." The teacher asks him, "More what?" Jared signs "more" again. The teacher signs "more drink" and gives a questioning look to Jared. Jared signs "more drink" and receives more juice.
Across Activities	Jared needs more blocks for the tower he is building. He asks the teacher for more toys and receives them.
Across People	Jared needs more blocks for the tower he is building. He asks the assistant teacher for more toys and receives them.
Across Materials	Jared has now asked for more juice and more of a variety of blocks.

Planning is a crucial factor to ensure that the potential benefits of embedded instruction are realized (Salisbury, Mangino, Petrigala, Rainforth, & Syryca, 1994; Santos, Lingnugaris/Kraft, & Akers, 1999; Wolery, 1994). In the remainder of this article we will describe a planning process for embedding learning opportunities. The focus of the planning process is to provide "user friendly," helpful materials to facilitate the use of embedding by individuals who are unfamiliar with the strategy or those who are partnering with educators who are new to the procedure. A three-step process is designed to aid the child's team in targeting objectives for embedding, identifying and creating opportunities to practice the learning objectives, ensuring multiple opportunities across the day, providing instructional support within these routines-based opportunities, and evaluating the impact of instruction on the child's learning. Each step will be fully described using Jared's preschool and IEP goals/objectives as illustration.

Step 1: "Dressing Up" the Learning Objective for the Preschool Curriculum

The purpose of this step is to translate ("dress up") a goal from a child's IEP to a learning objective that can be addressed effectively in the classroom. Here it is important to remember that learning objectives are not the same thing as activities; and planning an activity is not the same thing as providing instruction. For example, a child's objectives might include such skills as refined pincer grasp, matching, following two-step verbal commands, and putting two signs together to communicate requests. These objectives are not in themselves activities, but are skills that children are expected to use to more successfully participate in an activity. Thus the teacher begins by focusing on the activity and on embedding objectives or needed skills in ways that take advantage of natural cues, natural consequences, and opportunities for the child to use the skill across settings, materials, and people.

In addition, teachers must realize that the way in which an objective is written may actually limit the potential for embedding. For example, consider the objective of "object labeling" written as follows: *Child will correctly label four out of five pictures when asked, "What is this?"* It is likely that this objective will be taught by the teacher sitting at a table with the child and looking at pictures. But if the objective is written as *"Child will correctly label objects, a minimum of 80% of requests, when asked, "What is this?" within ongoing activities,"* the objective may be implemented by: (1) hiding objects in various places (e.g., in drawers, boxes) and encouraging labeling as each is "discovered," (2) labeling materials used in a "washing the baby" activity, (3) naming utensils and objects needed to set the table for snack time, or (4) when making choices. Thus, the first task in preparing for ELO is to target a learning objective or modify the established learning objective (i.e., for those children with an IEP) such that it can be easily and naturally embedded in multiple activities (e.g., water play, cooking, group games) and routines (e.g., arrival, snack, clean-up).

A shorthand reference for each child's program is an excellent tool to help the team discuss which objectives to target for embedding intervention and how they might be adapted to more readily fit into ongoing activities (Giangreco, Dennis, Edelman, & Cloninger, 1994). For example, Jared had objectives for developing a refined pincer grasp and improved eye-hand coordination. His team (mother, preschool teacher, early childhood special education itinerant teacher, and physical therapist) decided that these two objectives could be combined into one that requires using an efficient grasp and reach to pick up small materials, place items in containers, or remove them from containers. The "IEP-at-a-Glance" (See Table 2) adapted from Giangreco and colleagues (1994) provides brief descriptors of the objectives targeted, a brief description of the child's current abilities, and information on special management needs the child might require.

Step 2: Organizing the Objectives

To ensure that children progress on their embedded learning objectives, the teacher(s) need to ensure that sufficient opportunities are available across the day for the child to practice the objectives. This requires that the child's team use the IEP-at-a-Glance to carefully review each of the daily activities and routines to determine when opportunities naturally occur or could be easily modified to address each of the child's objectives. For example, Jared's team has noted that refining Jared's fine motor skills,

Table 2: IEP-at-a-Glance

Child's Name: __Jared_____ Age: __3____ Date: __9/01_____

Objectives Descriptors:	Child Profile:
• Two signs together • Pincer grasp/eye-hand coordination • Improving balance • Receptive language/following directions • Matching objects	Beginning to communicate verbally but continues to use sign language and verbal approximations (e.g., "wa" for water). Uses 25 single signs consistently (e.g., eat, drink, Mom, book, toy, want, stop, move, play, finish, sleep, cookie, water, out, music, computer, sing, cup, toothbrushing, open, mine, sit, push, dog, Dad). Can walk well but has problems transitioning across changes in elevation. Social interaction: mostly initiates interactions with adults; doesn't initiate well with peers; observes peers play; tends to play side by side. Greets and responds to greetings of familiar people.

Management Needs:

Uses grunts and pointing to communicate if not prompted to use signs. Can get easily frustrated and yells and stomps feet.

specifically a more efficient pincer grasp and eye-hand coordination in targeted reaching, is an important aspect of his learning objectives. The teacher makes careful notes about the various reaching and grasping opportunities occurring throughout the day (e.g., arrival and putting away belongings; toileting and self-care; picking up items during clean-up, snack time, etc.). She also notes any additional materials or modifications to activities necessary to increase the number of opportunities. For example, she noted that using "sliding lock" snack bags for small finger foods at snack time would not only require a refined grasp to remove the food from the bag but sliding the "lock" on the bag was yet another learning opportunity using slightly different movements.

To ensure sufficient practice opportunities across all of the child's objectives and activities during the day, it is often helpful for the classroom staff to utilize an individual child activity matrix. Use of an activity matrix for noting and organizing opportunities for addressing child objectives across daily routines and activities has been suggested and presented in the professional literature in early childhood special education for more than two decades. Notable examples include Doug Guess and colleagues' work on the "Individualized Curriculum Sequencing model" (Guess & Holovet, 1983); Diane Bricker and colleagues' work on "activity-based interventions" (Bricker et al., 1998); and Sarah Rule and colleagues' "daily teaching opportunities" (Rule, Utley, Qian, & Eastmond, 1999). The individual activity matrix is designed to describe and reflect the many opportunities to embed objectives throughout the daily program schedule. Table 3 provides an example activity matrix for Jared across several daily activity times in his preschool classroom.

Table 3: Individual Activity Matrix

Activity/ Time	Sign Combinations	Pincer Grasp/Eye-Hand Coordination	Improving Balance	Receptive Language: Following Directions	Matching
			Objectives to be Embedded		
Arrival	Greeting teacher, peers, saying good-bye to Mom	Hang coat on hook, place lunch bag in cubby, unzip book bag	Step up on cubby, climbing stairs to front door	As directions are needed to put away things and move into first activity	
Group	Responses to questions	Pick up items for finger play, musical instruments	Step over small obstacles on path to group circle	With pictures/ books/action songs (e.g., find the dog and the flower, tap your head and clap your hands)	Match colors, shapes as part of activity
Clean-Up	What to clean and where	Pick up materials and put in container	Squat to pick up items, use small step stool to place items on shelves	What to clean up and where to put it	Match objects to photos on shelves, match red blocks with red blocks in container, etc.
Toileting	"Go toilet," "I'm finished," "Want help"	Unzip pants, button pants	Climb stairs, jump down hallway from tile to tile, skip to toilet	Directions as needed	
Snack	Ask for items, ask for more items, ask for help opening items	Unzip snack bag, scoop food, pick up small crackers/foods		Directions as needed	Put items on place mat drawn with items

Step 3: Designing, Implementing, and Evaluating Embedded Instruction

Activities in and of themselves do not guarantee that children will make progress on their learning objectives even when these activities are fun and engaging. Further, creating an opportunity may not be sufficient for all the child's learning objectives. This is particularly the case if the goal represents a new behavior or one that requires more sophisticated behaviors than the child has currently in his or her repertoire. In these cases, the opportunity must be paired with instruction. Thus, once a matrix is completed, the child's team should review the objectives to determine which may require explicit instruction for the child to acquire the behavior.

If all or most of the objectives appear to require instruction, then the team may decide to prioritize and introduce the instruction in a staggered format to avoid overloading the classroom teaching staff. Further, prioritization can occur in identification of activities with which to focus the instruction. That is, the team may decide to provide instruction during two of the four activities/routines identified in the matrix. The other two activities provide for generalization opportunities. For example, Jared's teachers, together with the other members of the team, decided to target matching and fine motor. The team felt that the other skills were emerging and primarily required practice opportunities. All the team members felt strongly, however, that for Jared the two targets were new concepts and required a level of sophistication he did not yet demonstrate. Further, because Jared attends a child care program with 17 other children, the team decided to target activities in which additional help would be present or when the demand for teacher attention was less from the other children. Thus, clean-up and snack were targeted for instruction on his fine motor objective. During snack, a "floating" assistant was available to the class and so instruction could more easily occur. Similarly, snack was chosen for the matching task because of the additional staff present. Clean-up was identified as a time in which the other children did not require much assistance and therefore the teacher or her assistant could implement the instruction with Jared.

In designing good embedded instruction several key aspects must be addressed. The teacher must let the children know: (1) what they need to do, (2) how a "correct" response looks and feels, (3) the "correctness" of their response, and (4) that a response will result in a positive outcome. Thus, teachers must carefully plan how these aspects will be implemented to support the child's learning of each new skill. It also is critical that systematic monitoring of the child's progress occurs. It is

from this monitoring that teachers can determine when the child no longer needs their instructional support or when the plan requires modification because it is ineffective.

The "ELO-at-a-Glance" (adapted from McCormick & Feeney, 1995) is a useful organizing tool to accomplish these instructional planning components. To complete an ELO-at-a-Glance and plan for instruction on an objective the following four aspects must be determined: (1) *modifications needed* by the child to participate in the activity and for instruction on the objective to occur; (2) the teacher's instructional behaviors, i.e., determining *what you are going to do and say*, (3) what the consequence will be for the child accurately demonstrating the objective, i.e., *how you will respond*; and (4) the *evaluation procedures* that will be implemented. In the following sections, each aspect is briefly explained using the example ELO-at-a-Glance from Jared (Table 4) to illustrate.

Modifications Needed

First, the teacher determines what modifications must be included in the activity to create opportunities for learning the objective. This may involve adding materials (e.g., placemats for each child depicting a place for cups, plates, and napkins; multiple sets of items in same colors, as is the case for Jared) or removing materials (e.g., placing the glue for the art activity out of reach such that the child must ask for it); modifying the expectation for the activity (e.g., Jared becomes the helper who helps set the table); and/or designing the activity such that participation requires the use of the objective (e.g., Jared must match the items in order to complete the clean-up routine).

What Are You Going to Do and Say?

Next the teacher answers the guiding questions to plan how classroom staff will support the child's learning of the objective. First the question, "What are you going to do?" That is, how will one ensure that opportunities occur and that when they occur they are capitalized on as learning events? For example, Jared's teachers plan to let him know what is

Table 4: ELO-at-a-Glance for: __Jared__

Objective: __will correctly match a variety of everyday objects (e.g., class blocks, utensils, toy cars) by a single__
__visual attribute (e.g., color, shape, or size) 90% of recorded opportunities__

Date: __9/28__ Activity: __Snack=1 / Clean-Up=2__

Materials: __1=placemat / 2=same color toys/blocks__

(1) Modifications Needed:

1=Snack: Placemats for all children; Jared "helper" for a week for setting the table

2=Clean-Up: Multiple items of same color; have one item in bin or shelf with others out

(2a) What Are You Going to Do?

1=Provide initial model with first mat; give one item at a time with verbal prompt/cue; provide correction and "extra physical cuing" by tracing the outline of the item on the mat

2=Same as above, but in correction note color

(2b) What Are You Going to Say?

Use natural cues: "Let's see you do it."

"Place the cup here," as you trace the circle on the placemat and on the bottom of the cup

"Can you put all of the red cars in first?"

(3) How Will You Respond?

Praise; acknowledgment; feedback on accuracy; transition to next activity or next part of activity

(4) Evaluation Procedures:

Who? __Eva__   Where? __1=Snack / 2=1st & 2nd Clean-Up__

How? ____ Narrative Summary ____ Portfolio ____ Observation __X__ Counts

Keep a tally using the following coding scheme:

+ = independent correct   H = needs help (model, verbal prompt, physical prompt)

- = incorrect

When? __1=Tues. / 2=Thurs.__

9/4 (1) HHHHHHHHHHH   9/6 (2) HHHHHHHH

9/11 (1) HHH++-HHHHHH   9/13 (2) HHHHH+++

9/18 (1) H+++--HH-H-H   9/20 (2) +++++++++++

expected for table setting by completing the first step and thus modeling the correct response. They will also use natural conversation opportunities to encourage Jared to give it a try. Early on, to ensure that Jared understands what a correct response looks like, they may provide him with verbal prompts (e.g., "Put the cup on the circle," "Put this block with the other green ones") and physical cues (e.g., tracing the shape as verbal cues are provided to Jared to place the cup on the circle).

How Will You Respond?

Next, team members need to think about "How will you respond?" when the child produces the desired response (e.g., correctly matching objects by a single visual attribute 80% of recorded opportunities). The response must not only let the child know that he or she did the skill, but he or she must feel that the response was worth the effort. To enhance the likelihood that the child will want to do the skill again and again, the plan should include verbal feedback to the child on the accuracy of the response (e.g., the teacher says: "Yes, Jared that green car goes into the box with the other green toys"; while tracing the outline of the fork with her finger the teacher says, "Yes, Jared, the fork goes on the fork drawing"). If the child responds incorrectly, the teacher also must provide corrective feedback to the child (e.g., while tracing the outline of the fork on the placement and moving the fork from the plate outline the teacher says, "Look, Jared, the fork goes on the drawing of the fork"). Participation in an activity is an inherent reinforcement available when implementing embedded learning, however, teachers must ensure that participation is in fact a positive event. For Jared, completion of both activities allowed him to progress to the next routine. For example, upon finishing their clean-up activity all the children were allowed to look at a book in their cubby until everyone was finished. The quicker Jared completed the task, the sooner he was able to attend to his favorite book.

Evaluation Procedures

Finally, the teachers must decide how they are going to monitor the child's progress on his or her targeted objectives. This includes deciding who will be collecting the data and what format or procedure is best suited to the objective. In Jared's case the team thought the lead teacher could best record observed occurrences. Further, since matching is a relatively discrete skill (that is, it is readily observable and has a clear beginning and ending) keeping a running tally is an appropriate strategy. If a less discrete learning objective were targeted (such as using initiating and sustaining social interactions with peers), use of notes might be a better strategy. For learning objectives that produce a "product," such as "drawing vertical and horizontal lines," a portfolio in which dated samples with explanatory notes are reviewed across time would be appropriate. An excellent source for additional ideas and strategies for collecting progress data is Martin's (1998) *Take a Look: Observation and Portfolio Assessment in Early Childhood.*

Devising nonintrusive evaluation strategies that produce reliable information at a low cost can be a challenge. However, it is critical to good instruction. Furthermore, collecting information is only the first step to evaluating the success of this instructional strategy. The classroom team must examine the evaluation information regularly and make decisions based on this evaluation information. For example, Jared's data on matching shows that in three weeks of implementation, he has made wonderful progress during snack, but not clean-up. Could it be that the materials for clean-up are more difficult to discriminate? Is motivation a problem? Or could it be that adults are preempting his attempts to be independent because they are short on time? Although the evaluation data do not answer these questions, they do provide a lot of information about how to help Jared achieve his learning objective across materials and contexts.

Summary

Implementation of ELO is dependent on underlying structure and systematic planning to ensure that opportunities for learning objectives occur and that teachers capitalize on such opportunities. Teachable moments are created, recognized, and used to enhance a child's developmental progress. As with all good instruction, progress toward achieving learning objectives is monitored. Instructional decisions, such as progressing to more complex or next level skills or changing the instructional procedures, are made through careful analysis of data collected. The focus is on access to and participation in fun, enjoyable, and interesting activities for young children while making learning progress. Fun and meaningful activities provide the strongest motivation for young children to practice skills again and again throughout their day.

Notes

You can reach Eva Horn by e-mail at evahorn@ku.edu
Preparation of this manuscript and the research reported herein was supported through a grant from the U.S. Department of Education (HO24k40004).

References

Bricker, D., & Cripe, J. J. (1992). *An activity-based approach to early intervention.* Baltimore: Paul H. Brookes.

Bricker, D., Pretti-Frontczak, K., & McComas, N. R. (1998). *An activity-based approach to early intervention* (2nd ed.). Baltimore: Paul H. Brookes.

Fox, L., & Hanline, M. F. (1993). A preliminary evaluation of learning within developmentally appropriate early childhood settings. *Topics in Early Childhood Special Education, 13*(3), 308-327.

Giangreco, M., Dennis, R., Edelman, S., & Cloninger, C. (1994). Dressing your IEPs for the general education climate: Analysis of IEP goals and objectives for students with multiple disabilities. *Remedial and Special Education, 15*(5), 288-326.

Guess, D., & Holovet, J. (1983). *The Kansas Individualized Curriculum Sequence (ICS) model: Evaluation studies.* Lawrence, KS: University of Kansas.

Horn, E., Lieber, J., Sandall, S., Schwartz, I., & Li, S. (2000). Supporting young children's IEP goals in inclusive settings through embedded learning opportunities. *Topics in Early Childhood Special Education, 20*(4), 208-223.

Losardo, A., & Bricker, D. (1994). Activity-based and direct instruction: A comparison study. *American Journal of Mental Retardation, 98*(6), 744-765.

Martin, S. (1998). *Take a look: Observation and portfolio assessment in early childhood.* Don Mills, Ontario: Addison-Wesley.

McCormick, L., & Feeney, S. (1995). Modifying and expanding activities for children with disabilities. *Young Children, 50*(4), 10-17.

Mudd, J. M., & Wolery, M. (1987). Training Head Start teachers to use incidental teaching. *Journal of the Division for Early Childhood, 11*(2), 124-133.

Peck, C. A., Killen, C. C., & Baumgart, D. (1989). Increasing implementation of special education instruction in mainstream preschools: Direct and generalized effects of nondirective consultation. *Journal of Applied Behavior Analysis, 22*(2), 197-210.

Rule, S., Utley, G., Qian, A., & Eastmond, N. (1999). *Strategies for preschool intervention in everyday settings (SPIES) video series.* Logan, UT: Utah State University.

Salisbury, C. L., Mangino, M., Petrigala, M., Rainforth, B., & Syryca, S. (1994). Promoting the instructional inclusion of young children with disabilities in the primary grades. *Journal of Early Intervention, 18*(3), 311-322.

Sandall, S., Schwartz, I., Joseph, G., Chou, H. Y., Horn, E., Lieber, J., Odom, S., & Wolery, R. A. (in press). *Building blocks for successful early childhood programs: Strategies for including all children.* Baltimore: Paul H. Brookes.

Santos, R. M., Lingnugaris/Kraft, B., & Akers, J. (1999). Tips on planning center time activities for preschool classrooms. *Young Exceptional Children, 2*(4), 9-16.

Venn, M. L., & Wolery, M. (1992). Increasing daycare staff members' interactions during caregiving routines. *Journal of Early Intervention, 16*(4), 304-319.

Venn, M. L., Wolery, M., Werts, M. G., Morris, A., DeCesare, L. D., & Cuffs, M. S., (1993). Embedding instruction in art activities to teach preschoolers with disabilities to imitate their peers. *Early Childhood Research Quarterly, 8*(3), 277-294.

Wolery, M. (1994). Implementing instruction for young children with special needs in early childhood classrooms. In M. Wolery & J. S. Wilbers (Eds.), *Including children with special needs in early childhood programs* (pp. 97-118). Washington, DC: National Association for the Education of Young Children (NAEYC).

Wolery, M., & Wilbers, J. S. (Eds.). (1994). *Including children with special needs in early childhood programs.* Washington, DC: National Association for the Education of Young Children (NAEYC).

Using What Children Know to Teach Them Something New: Applying High-Probability Procedures in the Classroom and at Home

Rosa Milagros Santos, Ph.D., University of Illinois at Urbana-Champaign

Adrian, a three-year old, is Alex and Angie's first child. Diagnosed with developmental delays, he has shown remarkable progress in his language and motor skills since he began receiving early intervention services last year. At his recent Individualized Family Service Plan (IFSP) meeting, one of Adrian's daycare teachers, an early intervention (EI) service coordinator, and his parents agreed that they need to help him follow through on specific adult requests such as putting away his toys. At home, Angie engages in a drawn-out struggle with Adrian to get him to put away his toys before bedtime. Most of the time, Adrian ends up in time-out while Angie puts away his toys.

In addition, his daycare teacher reported that Adrian does not usually verbally respond to comments and conversations initiated by his teachers and peers. While he responds to a teacher's direct requests (e.g., "What is this?"), they also want Adrian to learn to respond to indirect requests that often occur in the classroom (e.g., silly comments or unexpected events). It was suggested at the meeting that they try an intervention strategy that builds on skills that Adrian has mastered to teach him new skills—such as putting away his toys and responding to his teachers' indirect requests—called high-probability procedures.

Current DEC recommended practices suggest the use of high-probability procedures as one of many strategies early childhood special education teachers can use to "... increase the complexity and duration of children's play, engagement, appropriate behavior, and learning" (Wolery, 2000, p. 37). The purpose of this article is to define high-probability procedures, describe the components of this intervention strategy, and suggest some issues to consider in choosing to use high-probability procedures.

High-Probability Procedures Defined

High-probability procedures use requests by adults for skills that are already in the child's repertoire prior to requesting that the child perform new skills. Skills in the child's repertoire are those that the child can easily and consistently perform. These are skills for which the probability of the child performing the skill in response to an adult request (e.g., "Touch your toes" or "Tell me your name") is very high, hence the term "high-probability requests" or "high-p." New skills are those that the child has difficulty performing on a consistent basis and thus the probability of the child performing the request is low, hence the term "low-probability requests" or "low-p." For the purposes of this article, the term "high-probability procedures" refers to strategies that consist of an adult delivering a series of requests, in most research studies three consecutive requests, to which a child responds consistently (high-p) immediately before delivering a request to which the child does not respond consistently (low-p). When children are presented with a series of requests to which they are likely to respond, their rate of responding increases. This often results in an increased rate of reinforcement. The response rate and reinforcement rate creates a "momentum" that increases the likelihood of children responding to low-p requests (Santos & Lignugaris/Kraft, 1999).

Research on High-Probability Procedures

Much has been written about high-probability procedures and its effectiveness in increasing compliance of school-age children and adults with and without disabilities (e.g., Davis, Brady, Williams, & Hamilton, 1992; Davis et al., 1994; Ducharme & Worling, 1994; Horner et al., 1991; Houlihan, Jacobson, & Brandon, 1994; Mace et al., 1990; Sanchez-Fort, Brady, & Davis, 1995; Singer, Singer, & Horner, 1987; Wehby & Hollahan, 2000; Zarcone, Iwata, Mazaleski, & Smith, 1994). In the literature, high-probability procedures have been labeled as "high-probability requests" (Harchik & Putzier, 1990; Zarcone, Iwata, Mazaleski, & Smith, 1994); "behavioral momentum" (Davis & Brady, 1993; Mace et al., 1990; Nevin, Mandell, & Atak, 1983; Nevin, Tota, Torquato, & Shull, 1990); "pretask requests" (Singer, Singer, & Horner, 1987); and "interspersed requests" (Horner, Day, Sprague, O'Brien, & Heathfield, 1991). Recent research on high-probability procedures suggests the efficacy of these procedures with young children as well (Davis & Brady, 1993; Davis & Reichle, 1996; Houlihan, Jacobson, & Brandon, 1994; Killu et al., 1998; McComas, Wacker, & Cooper, 1998; Rortvedt & Miltenberger, 1994).

Furthermore, researchers suggest (Davis & Brady, 1993; Santos & Lignugaris/Kraft, 1999) that high-probability procedures can be used to address specific skills such as motor and language development of preschoolers with disabilities. In two related studies, high-probability procedures were used to teach preschool children with language delays new "color" words (Lignugaris/Kraft & Santos, 1997) and to increase their responding to teachers' indirect questions and silly comments (Santos & Lignugaris/Kraft, 1999). What is interesting about these studies is how high-probability procedures were embedded in the children's classroom routines and activities. Additionally, naturalistic teaching procedures recommended by DEC " ... to promote acquisition and use of communication and social skills" (Wolery, 2000, p. 37) were easily and successfully combined with high-probability procedures. For example, Santos and Lignugaris/Kraft (1999) combined high-probability procedures with a mand-model procedure wherein the teacher asked the child a " ... non-yes/no question or an instruction to verbalize" (Warren, McQuarter, & Rogers-Warren, 1984, p. 45). Results from these studies suggest that the children acquired the new skills when high-probability procedures were introduced. And, they suggest the potential utility of high-probability procedures to teach children a variety of skills.

Given the increased interest in the use of high-probability procedures with young children with disabilities and current recommendations to the field for its use as an intervention strategy, it is important for teachers and other practitioners to learn how to apply these procedures in their respective settings. Parents and caregivers may also take interest in this procedure to use with children at home.

Applying High-Probability Procedures in the Classroom and at Home

Using high-probability procedures in the classroom or at home can be easy. To be effective, careful observation and planning are necessary. There are three components involved in effectively implementing high-probability procedures. Following is a description of each of the components with corresponding examples and some helpful hints.

Component 1: Determine the High-*P* and Low-*P* Requests

For the high-probability procedures to work, the adult must first identify high-*p* requests to which the child will likely respond consistently and fluently, then target a low-*p* request to which the adult wants the child to begin responding (i.e., one that the child does not respond to currently or responds to inconsistently). The child's consistent and correct responding to high-*p* requests is very important as it creates momentum and thus increases the probability that the child will respond to the low-*p* request.

Both high-*p* and low-*p* requests may require a motor or language response from the child. For example, when transitioning from one activity to the next, the teacher may ask the child to pick up toys, to put on his or her coat, or to get his or her book bag. When conversing with a child during typical routines or activities (e.g., snack or story time) the teacher's request may require the child to respond vocally or use sign language. For example, the teacher may ask the child to label specific objects (e.g., "What did you make?"), to select from a choice of items (e.g., "Would you like an apple or a banana?"), or to describe items (e.g., "What color is your shirt?") or events/activities (e.g., "What does the cat say?").

Adrian can identify objects such as body parts when asked (e.g., "What is this?" or "Where is Mr. Bear's ear?"). Angie, his mother, knows that he responds to these requests more than 80% of the time. Adrian, however, has difficulty responding to his mother's specific request to put away his toys after he is done playing with them. In this situation, Angie can use labeling objects as her high-*p* requests to encourage Adrian to begin responding to her low-*p* request of putting away his toys (e.g., "Let's put your toys in the box.").

At child care, Adrian's teachers know that he readily responds to direct requests to label objects found in their classroom (e.g., "What do you need?" or "What did you make?"). They decide to use direct requests as their high-*p* to encourage Adrian to respond to their low-*p* request of responding to an indirect request (e.g., a silly comment such as, "That's a dog" while referring to a cat).

Component 2: Use Routines, Activities, and Materials in the Child's Environment

DEC recommends the " ... use [of] systematic procedures within and across environments, activities, and routines to promote children's learning and participation" (Wolery, 2000, p. 37). Planning is the key to embedding high-probability procedures within typically occurring routines and activities, using high interest materials in the child's environment. For example, teachers often know which toys and materials the child plays with most while in the classroom. Additionally, observing the child allows a teacher to determine preferred routines and activities. These high interest materials, routines, and activities should be incorporated into high-probability procedures.

On weekdays, Angie routinely plays with Adrian when she returns home from work, when she gives him a bath, and before she puts him to bed. During these times, Adrian selects toys to play with his mother. Lately, Angie has noticed that Adrian plays more with toys that he can put together and pull apart such as Duplo® blocks and Mr. Potato Head®. Adrian also enjoys the various art activities at child care: using materials such as markers, paint, glue, construction paper, and crayons. His teachers notice that when these materials are readily available, Adrian eagerly goes to the art area to use them to create pictures to bring home. Using toys, materials, and activities that Adrian likes during typical routines at home and in school will help Angie and his teachers implement high-probability procedures with ease.

Component 3: Deliver Three High-*P* Requests and One Low-*P* Request

The actual implementation of high-probability procedures is often brief, usually taking place in between one to two minutes within an activity. Teachers have used the procedure as a game, akin to Simon Says. For example, to get children to sit on the floor for a large group activity, a teacher can deliver a series of high-*p* requests (e.g., "Pat your shoulders," "Wiggle your ears," "Jump up as high as you can") and then deliver the low-*p* request ("OK, sit on the floor!").

High-probability procedures also can be implemented along with other teaching strategies that are embedded within the child's typically occurring activities and routines, such as incidental teaching, mand-model procedures, milieu teaching, and language expansion. An example of a combination of high-probability procedures and other teaching strategies is provided in Table 1 (Adrian and his mother) and Table 2 (Adrian and his teacher).

Table 1: Sample of High-Probability Procedures Applied at Home

Setting: Adrian and his mother, Angie, are playing with Mr. Potato Head®. Angie uses high-probability procedures to encourage Adrian to follow her request to put away his toys so that they can get ready for bed.

	High-*p* Request	High-*p* Request	High-*p* Request	Low-*p* Request
Angie makes **requests:**	"Adrian, find Mr. Potato Head's nose for me."	"Have you seen Mr. Potato Head's hat?"	"May I have Mr. Potato Head's shoes?"	"Help me put Mr. Potato Head back in his box."
Adrian **responds** to his mother's requests:	Adrian hands the nose to his mother.	Adrian hands the hat to his mother.	Adrian hands the shoes to his mother.	Adrian hands Mr. Potato Head parts to his mother to put back in the box.
Angie **praises** Adrian for responding to her requests:	"That's great! You found his nose!"	"That's right, that's his baseball cap!"	"Good job! You found his yellow shoes."	"Thanks for putting your toys away, son!"

Table 2: Sample of High-Probability Procedures Applied in the Classroom

Setting: In Adrian's child care, his teacher uses high-probability procedures during tabletop activities to encourage Adrian to respond consistently to her comments.

	High-*p* Request	High-*p* Request	High-*p* Request	Low-*p* Request
His teacher makes **requests:**	"Adrian, what are you making?"	"Who's that?"	"What's that on top of the house?"	"That looks like a *yellow* bird" (silly comment)
Adrian **responds** to his teacher's requests:	"My house!"	"Adrian and Mommy."	"A birdie."	"No, it's a red bird!"
His teacher **praises** Adrian for responding to her requests:	"Oh, that's a big house."	"That's really nice."	"You drew a pretty bird."	"Oh that's right, it is a *red* bird!"

Adrian's mother uses the teaching strategy "systematic commenting" along with the high-probability procedures by providing a descriptor and label for each of the items that Adrian hands her (e.g., "yellow shoes"). Adrian's teacher uses the teaching strategy "language expansion" wherein she extends Adrian's verbalizations by elaborating on his responses to her direct questions (e.g., the teacher asks,

"What's this?" Adrian responds, "my house," and his teacher elaborates, "*big* house"). Further, if Adrian needs assistance to become more fluent with the target skill, high-probability procedures can easily be combined with adult models or physical or verbal assistance. For example, if Adrian responds incorrectly to his mother's low-*p* request, "Let's put away your toys," then Angie can use a physical prompt by placing her hand over Adrian's as they pick up the toys. She can pair this with a verbal cue, "This is how we put away your toys." Adrian's teacher can model the correct response following an incorrect response to her low-*p* request by saying, for example, "Oh, how silly, that isn't yellow, it's a *red* bird! Can you say red?"

The delivery of three high-*p* requests prior to the delivery of the low-*p* request has been the standard in most research studies that have produced promising effects (e.g., Davis & Reichle, 1996; Santos & Lignugaris/Kraft, 1999). The key, however, is in the timing of the delivery of the high-*p* and low-*p* requests and reinforcing the child (e.g., by giving verbal praise). To build momentum, a sequence of three high-*p* requests are delivered in rapid succession immediately followed by the low-*p* request. Research studies (Davis & Brady, 1993; Davis & Reichle, 1996; Davis, Reichle, Southard, & Johnston, 1998; Houlihan, Jacobson, & Brandon, 1994) suggest delivering the low-*p* request five seconds after the correct response to the third high-*p* request. Finally, appropriately praise and reinforce each correct response in the sequence (whether done independently or requiring adult assistance).

Final Considerations

As with almost any intervention procedure, high-probability procedures may not work for all children, across all situations. Santos and Lignugaris/Kraft (1999) noted situations in which high-probability procedures may not be as effective. First, children's behavior and dispositions may impact their compliance to any type of adult request. Some children, for a bevy of reasons, may exhibit challenging behaviors that could run counter to high-probability procedures. A power struggle could occur between the child and the adult during interactions, which may substantially reduce the child's responses to the adult's requests. For example, Adrian might respond inconsistently by only following through on every other high-*p* request delivered by his mother or his teachers. Or, Adrian might simply refuse to respond to his mother's or his teachers' high-*p* requests. In both cases, Angie or Adrian's teachers would be unable to create the momentum necessary to prompt Adrian to respond to the low-*p* request of putting his toys away or sitting down,

for example. In such situations, it is best to first address other behaviors that may counteract the effective implementation of high-probability procedures.

Second, it is important that the child can consistently and correctly respond to the high-p requests. If the child is responding but is giving incorrect responses, this would result in less reinforcement as the adult would likely use correction procedures. For example, if Adrian incorrectly hands Angie a part she has requested, she might say instead, "Oh, those are Mr. Potato Head®'s eyes; give me his hat." Until Adrian hands her the correct item, Angie is not able to deliver the next request and therefore is unable to build Adrian's momentum to respond. As noted previously, increasing the rate of reinforcement, which is a result of increased responding to high-p requests, is necessary to build the momentum to respond to low-p requests.

Third, the presence of other children may impact the child's responsiveness to the requests. If the request requires a verbal response, other children eager to respond to the teacher or caregiver may respond before or on behalf of the specific child being targeted for the high-probability procedures. In this situation, it is recommended to plan the grouping of the children so that the target child is with peers who likely would not preempt his or her response to the request. For specific motor skills, being with peers who can "play the game" may benefit the target child, either to provide a model for the correct response or to engage him or her to participate with the rest of the class. For example, Adrian enjoys action songs that involve interacting with his peers (e.g., patting each other's shoulder or holding hands).

Finally, high-probability procedures are best used as a short-term intervention. Most research studies using these procedures (e.g., Davis et al., 1998; Killu et al., 1998; Santos & Lignugaris/Kraft, 1999) have demonstrated that the effects of this strategy are immediate. For example, once Adrian consistently responds to his mother's request to put away his toys (low-p), Angie could begin to rely on natural cues and consequences. For some children, the "game" can become repetitive, predictable, and tiresome, which could result in them exhibiting challenging behaviors as a means to escape or avoid having to respond to the adult all the time.

High-probability procedures can be easily and effectively implemented in the classroom and at home. Research on these procedures has demonstrated promising and efficient results in addressing a multitude of skills. Implementing the procedures requires careful planning to identify the skills that will be used (high-*p*) and to teach the new skill(s) (low-*p*) during typical routines and activities using high interest materials. High-probability procedures can be implemented within a very short period of time and can potentially yield powerful results.

Note

You can reach Rosa Milagros Santos by e-mail at rsantos@uiuc.edu

References

Davis, C. A., & Brady, M. P. (1993). Expanding the utility of behavioral momentum: Where we've been, where we need to go. *Journal of Early Intervention, 17*(3), 211-223.

Davis, C. A., Brady, M. P., Hamilton, R., McEvoy, M. A., & Williams, R. E. (1994). Effects of high-probability requests on the social interactions of young children with behavior disorders. *Journal of Applied Behavior Analysis, 27*(4), 619-637.

Davis, C. A., Brady, M. P., Williams, R. E., & Hamilton, R. (1992). Effects of high-probability requests on the acquisition and generalization of responses to requests in young children with behavior disorders. *Journal of Applied Behavior Analysis, 25*(4), 905-916.

Davis, C. A., & Reichle, J. (1996). Variant and invariant high-probability requests: Increasing appropriate behaviors in children with emotional-behavioral disorders. *Journal of Applied Behavior Analysis, 29*(4), 471-482.

Davis, C. A., Reichle, J., Southard, K., & Johnston, S. (1998). Teaching children with severe disabilities to utilize nonobligatory conversational opportunities: An application of high-probability requests. *Journal of the Association for Persons With Severe Handicaps, 23*(1), 57-68.

Ducharme, J. M., & Worling, D. E. (1994). Behavioral momentum and stimulus fading in the acquisition and maintenance of child compliance in the home. *Journal of Applied Behavior Analysis, 27*(4), 639-647.

Harchik, A. E., & Putzier, V. S. (1990). The use of high-probability requests to increase compliance with instructions to take medication. *Journal of the Association for Persons With Severe Handicaps, 15*(1), 40-43.

Horner, R. H., Day, H. M., Sprague, J. R., O'Brien, M., & Heathfield, L. T. (1991). Interspersed requests: A nonaversive procedure for reducing aggression and self-injury during instruction. *Journal of Applied Behavior Analysis, 24*(2), 265-278.

Houlihan, D., Jacobson, L., & Brandon, P. K. (1994). Replication of a high-probability request sequence with varied interprompt times in a preschool setting. *Journal of Applied Behavior Analysis, 27*(4), 737-738.

Killu, K., Sainato, D. M., Davis, C. A., Ospelt, H., & Paul, J. N. (1998). Effects of high-probability request sequences on preschoolers' compliance and disruptive behavior. *Journal of Behavioral Education, 8*(4), 347-368.

Lignugaris/Kraft, B., & Santos, R. M. (1997). *The effects of high-probability requests on children's responses to low-probability requests.* Unpublished manuscript, Utah State University.

Mace, F. C., Lalli, J. S., Shea, M. C., Lalli, E. P., West, B. J., Roberts, M., & Nevin, J. A. (1990). The momentum of human behavior in a natural setting. *Journal of the Experimental Analysis of Behavior, 54*(3), 163-172.

McComas, J. J., Wacker, D. P., & Cooper, L. J. (1998). Increasing compliance with medical procedures: Application of the high-probability request procedures to a toddler. *Journal of Applied Behavior Analysis, 31*(2), 287-290.

Nevin, J. A., Mandell, C. E., & Atak, J. R. (1983). The analysis of behavioral momentum. *Journal of the Experimental Analysis of Behavior, 39*(1), 49-59.

Nevin, J. A., Tota, M. E., Torquato, R. D., & Shull, R. L. (1990). Alternative reinforcement increased resistance to change: Pavlovian or operant contingencies? *Journal of the Experimental Analysis of Behavior, 53*(3), 359-379.

Rortvedt, A. K., & Miltenberger, R. G. (1994). Analysis of a high-probability instructional sequence and time-out treatment of child noncompliance. *Journal of Applied Behavior Analysis, 27*(2), 327-330.

Sanchez-Fort, M. R., Brady, M. P., & Davis, C. A. (1995). Using high-probability requests to increase low-probability communication behavior in young children with severe disabilities. *Education and Training in Mental Retardation and Developmental Disabilities, 6*(2), 151-165.

Santos, R. M., & Lignugaris/Kraft, B. (1999). The effects of direct questions on preschool children's responses to indirect requests. *Journal of Behavioral Education, 9*(3/4), 193-210.

Singer, G. H., Singer, J., & Horner, R. H. (1987). Using pretask requests to increase the probability of compliance for students with severe disabilities. *Journal of the Association for Persons With Severe Handicaps, 12*(4), 287-291.

Warren, S. F., McQuarter, R. J., & Rogers-Warren, A. K. (1984). The effects of mands and models on the speech of unresponsive language-delayed preschool children. *Journal of Speech and Hearing Disorders, 37*(2), 43-52.

Wehby, J. H., & Hollahan, M. S. (2000). Effects of high-probability requests on the latency to initiate academic tasks. *Journal of Applied Behavior Analysis, 33*(2), 259-262.

Wolery, M. (2000). Recommended practices in child-focused interventions. In S. Sandall, M. E. McLean, & B. J. Smith (Eds.), *DEC recommended practices in early intervention/early childhood special education* (pp. 29-37). Longmont, CO: Sopris West.

Zarcone, J. R., Iwata, B. A., Mazaleski, J. L., & Smith, R. G. (1994). Momentum and extinction effects on self-injurious escape behavior and noncompliance. *Journal of Applied Behavior Analysis, 27*(4), 649-658.

Embedding Time Delay Procedures in Classroom Activities

Mark Wolery, Ph.D., Vanderbilt University

Isaiah is a three-year old boy with autism enrolled in an inclusive class. Goals for Isaiah are to use words to request, to use words for objects and actions, to initiate proximity with his peers, to give objects to peers, to push down and pull up his pants at toileting, and to increase the duration of his play. He imitates adults, requests non-verbally, plays with a few toys, has some stereotypic behavior, and is fairly compliant. His class has nine children (three with and six without disabilities), a teacher, and two assistants. Isaiah follows the same activity schedule as his classmates; no pull-out therapy is used. His teachers and parents want his goals addressed within the usual classroom activities and routines.

Two Division for Early Childhood (DEC) recommendations (Sandall, McLean, & Smith, 2000) will be useful to his teachers: (1) "prompting and prompt fading procedures (e.g., modeling, graduated guidance, increasing assistance, time delay) are used to ensure acquisition and use of communicative, self-care, cognitive, and social skills"; and (2) "specialized procedures (e.g., naturalistic strategies and prompt/prompt fading strategies) are embedded and distributed within and across activities" (Wolery, 2000, p. 37). This article describes constant and progressive time delay and how to embed and distribute time delay procedures into classroom activities.

What Is Time Delay?

Time delay comes in three versions: constant (Wolery, Ault, & Doyle, 1992), progressive (Wolery, Ault, & Doyle, 1992), and naturalistic (Schwartz, Anderson, & Halle, 1989). Each version (explained later) uses prompts (i.e., help, assistance) and, over time, the removal of those prompts so children perform independently. *Prompts* are what adults do

to give children information about how to do skills. Prompts may be physical (e.g., hand-over-hand, nudges), models, verbal hints and cues, gestures, or pictures. Time delay uses a special prompt called a controlling prompt. *Controlling prompts* give children enough help to perform the desired behavior correctly. Models are often controlling prompts, when children imitate adults. Physical prompts are often controlling prompts for nonimitative children. When controlling prompts are used, children can do the skill. Time delay also uses *task cues* such as questions (e.g., "What's this?"), commands (e.g., "Give me the ___," "Say ___"), or natural situations (e.g., pulling up pants after toileting).

Time delay uses two types of teaching trials: 0-second trials and delay trials. The 0-second trials are used in the first two or three days of teaching a new skill, and then the delay trials are used. For *0-second trials*, the adult gives the task cue, immediately gives the prompt, gives the child a chance to do the skill (i.e., the response interval), and then reinforces correct responses or ignores errors. *Response intervals* are usually three to five seconds long. For *delay trials*, the adult gives the task cue, gives a response interval, gives the prompt if the child did not respond, gives another response interval, and then gives the consequences. With time delay, the adult reinforces correct responses before *and* after the prompt. For example, when Isaiah's teacher uses delay trials when teaching him to use words to name toys, she would say, "What's this?" and wait the delay interval. If Isaiah answered correctly before the prompt, she would praise him and let him continue playing (reinforcer). If, however, he answered correctly after the prompt, she would still praise him and let him continue playing (reinforcer). The adult ignores no responses and errors after the prompt. For errors before the prompt, the adult says something such as, "Wait and I will show you."

The three time delay versions all use 0-second trials first. But they differ in how delay trials are used. With *constant time delay*, the response intervals of delay trials are all of the same length. With *progressive time delay*, the response intervals gradually increase over trials or days. For example, after two days of 0-second trials, the response interval on the third day may be one second; on the fourth, two seconds; on the fifth, three seconds; and so forth. Usually, the response interval should be no longer than five or six seconds. *Naturalistic time delay* is similar to the other two procedures, but it is used in routines at the point at which the child often receives assistance.

What Are Embedding and Distributing?

Embedding and distributing refer to when teaching trials are given. *Embedded* means the trials are used in naturally occurring activities and routines (Wolery, 1994). *Distributed* means the child has opportunities to perform other behaviors between trials on a given skill (Mulligan, Guess, Holvoet, & Brown, 1980). For example, to teach Isaiah to use words when requesting, his teacher embedded learning opportunities into snack by giving him only small portions of juice and food. She distributed the opportunities for requesting within snack time by having Isaiah eat and drink between requests.

There are several reasons for using embedded and distributed teaching. Using these procedures, children with disabilities can be taught during the same activities as their classmates. This minimizes the need for special one-to-one sessions. Skills also can be taught when they are needed and are related to the child's play or attention (Bricker, Pretti-Frontczak, & McComas, 1998). This helps promote generalization (i.e., use of the skill when and where it is needed), because teaching happens during the usual flow of the day. Use of distributed teaching also is supported by basic research with different types of learners (Mulligan et al., 1980). Finally, in practice, distributed teaching appears to be superior to massed-trial teaching (i.e., sessions in which trials on a behavior are presented repeatedly with little time for other behavior between trials) (Doyle, Wolery, Ault, Gast, & Wiley, 1989; Dunlap, 1984).

Is Time Delay Effective When it Is Embedded and Distributed?

Constant and progressive time delay were evaluated in many studies using one-to-one and small group instruction (Wolery, Ault, & Doyle, 1992). These studies show that constant and progressive time delay work with preschoolers and older children. The procedures work with children who do not have disabilities. They are effective for children with language delays, developmental delays, significant disabilities, mental retardation, and autism. They are effective for teaching discrete behaviors such as answering questions and labeling pictures, and for skills with many steps such as putting on a coat or using a spoon (Schuster et al., 1998). Naturalistic time delay also is effective with many communicative skills (Schwartz, Anderson, & Halle, 1989).

Eight studies evaluated constant and progressive time delay when they were embedded and distributed. They found that time delay is effective when embedded and distributed into free play (Chiara, Schuster, Bell, & Wolery, 1995), independent seatwork in an elementary class (Caldwell, Wolery, Werts, & Caldwell, 1996), teacher-directed instruction (Wolery, Anthony, Snyder, Werts, & Katzenmeyer, 1997), transitions between activities (Wolery, Anthony, & Heckathorn, 1998), and art activities (Venn et al., 1993). In these studies, the teachers were able, with some training, to use the procedures accurately. The embedded and distributed teaching did not interfere with the teachers' ability to carry out their classroom duties. Each study occurred in inclusive classes, except for the independent seatwork study (Caldwell et al., 1996). All the studies resulted in learning. One exception was when constant time delay was embedded into transitions; two children with oppositional behaviors did not learn well (Werts, Wolery, Venn, Demblowski, & Doren, 1996; Wolery, Anthony, & Heckathorn, 1998).

Steps for Embedding and Distributing Time Delay in Activities

Ten steps are described following for embedding and distributing time delay into classroom activities. The child, Isaiah, described in the vignette, is used to illustrate the steps; see also Table 1.

Table 1: Example Plan to Embed and Distribute Time Delay for Isaiah

| Steps for Using Time Delay | Isaiah's Goals to be Taught by Embedding and Distributing Time Delay | | |
	Using Words to Request	Using Words for Actions	Getting Pants Up and Down at Toileting
Step 1: Identify the skills to be taught	Naming food and drink items. Using "Want __" or "__, please" forms. Naming toys when given the choice between two.	Naming actions he is doing (e.g., stacking, riding, pounding, pushing, sliding, driving, cooking)	Grasping side of pants, pushing pants down to ankles; grasping pants in front and back and pulling pants up over buttocks
Step 2: Identify the activities and routines for teaching	Snack, lunch, and when given a choice of toys during free play	Free play and during play on the playground	Toileting routines— when he sits on the toilet

continued

Steps for Using Time Delay	Isaiah's Goals to be Taught by Embedding and Distributing Time Delay		
	Using Words to Request	Using Words for Actions	Getting Pants Up and Down at Toileting
Step 3: Decide how many and how often trials will be used	Every time he makes a nonverbal request by reaching for an item, moving an adult's hand, or holding up his cup	10 times per day. At least 2 minutes between trials and no more than 10 minutes	About 4 times per day; every time he sits on the toilet
Step 4: Select a time delay procedure	Constant time delay	Progressive time delay	Constant time delay
Step 5: Identify a task cue and controlling prompt	His nonverbal requests and any choice he is given; prompt is verbal model	"What are you doing?"; prompt is verbal model	Standing in front of the toilet; prompt is physical (hand-over-hand)
Step 6: Select a reinforcer	Getting the item he requested	Continuing to play and praise that uses the word he said	Praise and about a minute of interaction with the adult
Step 7: Determine the number of 0-second trials to use	2 days of 0-second trials	4 days of 0-second trials	3 days of 0-second trials
Step 8: Determine the length of the response interval	4 seconds	Increase by 1-second increments every 2 days; stop at 5 seconds	4 seconds
Step 9: Select and use a monitoring system	Count number of requests, number of verbal requests before prompt and after prompt, number of nonverbal requests before and after prompt	Count number of questions, number of action words before and after prompt, number of errors before and after prompt, and number of no responses	Count number of steps correct before the prompt and number of steps wrong before prompt
Step 10: Implement the plan and monitor its use and effects	Keep track of how many requests occur and whether the steps of time delay were done correctly	Keep track of how many questions were asked and whether the steps of time delay were done correctly	Keep track of the number of toileting routines in which he was taught and whether the steps of time delay were done correctly

Step 1: Identify the Skills to be Taught

Time delay is designed to teach specific skills; so, you must identify the skills to be taught. Time delay can be used for skills from each developmental domain. For Isaiah, the teachers will use time delay for three skills: (1) using words when requesting, (2) using action words to describe his play, and (3) pushing down and pulling up his pants during toileting routines.

Step 2: Identify the Activities and Routines for Teaching

Embedding and distributing are more likely to occur if you identify activities and routines for each goal. The procedures may be implemented during a single activity (Venn et al., 1993), multiple activities (Chiara et al., 1995), or during transitions between activities (Werts et al., 1996). Deciding when to embed time delay depends on what you are teaching, how many teaching opportunities are possible, and your other responsibilities. Isaiah's teachers will teach using words to request during snacks and meals and when he is given choices in structured free play. They will teach him to use action words during free play and outdoor play. They will teach him to push down and pull up his pants during toileting routines.

Step 3: Decide How Many and How Often Trials Will be Used

You must balance giving the child enough opportunities to learn the skill and carrying out the actual activities. Children often need approximately five trials per day for each skill being taught, but this number varies for different children. A minimum and maximum time between trials can be set (e.g., at least two minutes between trials but no more than ten). For Isaiah, using words to request will be taught each time he requests nonverbally or is given a choice. If Isaiah does not make a request in three minutes, an adult will ask him if he wants something. For action words, his teachers will use the "at least two minutes but no more than ten" rule. Teaching of pushing down and pulling up his pants will occur each time Isaiah goes to the bathroom.

Step 4: Select a Time Delay Procedure

Both constant and progressive time delay are effective and result in rapid learning (Ault, Gast, & Wolery, 1988). Constant time delay is somewhat easier to use, but you should make a choice between them based on the child. If the child waits for help and is attentive, then use the constant time delay procedure. If the child has difficulty waiting, use the progressive procedure to better ensure child success. With Isaiah, his teachers will use constant time delay when teaching him to use words to request, because he attends and waits for what he wants. For using action words, his teachers will use the progres-  sive time delay procedure because Isaiah will be involved in his play. For pushing down and pulling up his pants, they will use a constant time delay procedure because Isaiah waits well in that situation.

Step 5: Identify a Task Cue and Controlling Prompt

The task cue is something that lets children know they should perform the behavior being taught. This may be a question, command, or naturally occurring situation. The task cue is what begins a trial for the adult and child. For Isaiah, the requests he initiates (a naturally occurring situation) will be the task cue for using words to make requests. For using action words, the task cue will be an adult asking, "What are you doing?" For dressing during toileting, standing in front of the toilet (a naturally occurring situation) will be the task cue. Controlling prompts give children enough information so they can perform the behavior being taught. For Isaiah, the prompt will be a verbal model for using words to request (e.g., "Want milk") and using action words (e.g., "riding," "running"). Verbal models are used because he imitates adults. Physical prompts will be used for the toileting routines.

Step 6: Select a Reinforcer

Time delay requires the use of reinforcers, which must be selected individually for each child. Almost anything—such as continuing an activity, brief interactions with adults, or toys—can be reinforcers. An advantage of embedding instruction is that the naturally occurring activities (if fun and interesting to the child) may be in and of themselves reinforcers. This may explain why embedding and distributing are effective. For Isaiah, receiving the food, drink, or toy he requests is the reinforcer for using words to request. Continuing to play and praise are reinforcers for using action words. Adult interaction is the reinforcer for pushing down and pulling up his pants during toileting routines.

Step 7: Determine the Number of 0-Second Trials to Use

The 0-second trials build the relationship between the task cue and the skill being taught. On these trials, the adult prompts the child to perform the behavior correctly and then gives the reinforcer. This teaches the child the relationship between the task cue and the skill. This relationship is critical; give plenty of 0-second trials. Two or three days are often sufficient, but up to five days is fine. With Isaiah, his teachers will provide two days of 0-second trials at snack and lunch, and four days of these trials for using action words. More days of 0-second trials are used for action words because more words are being taught and because Isaiah may be focused on his play. For managing his pants, three days will be used because the skill is difficult.

Step 8: Determine the Length of the Response Interval

Usually the time the teacher waits for the child to respond is three to five seconds long. This gives the child time to start the skill, but the child does not have to wait long if he or she does not know what to do. After the 0-second trials with constant time delay, the length of the response interval does not change. With progressive time delay, the response interval length gradually increases. Increase the interval by one or two seconds every two or three days. If the child is slow to respond, make the response interval longer. To time the length of the interval, silently count "1001, 1002, etc." With Isaiah, the response interval for using words to request and for managing his pants will be four seconds. For using action words, the interval will be increased by one second every two days.

Step 9: Select and Use a Monitoring System

You must use a systematic method to track child progress and to make decisions about how to change your teaching, if necessary. With time delay, the child can do three things on the 0-second trials: (1) be correct, (2) be wrong, or (3) not respond. During 0-second trials, if the child is wrong on 25% or more for two or more days, then you should use a more controlling prompt. If the child does not respond to 25% or more trials for two or more days, then select a better reinforcer (Wolery, Ault, & Doyle, 1992).

With the delay trials, the child can do one of five things: (1) be correct *before* the prompt, (2) be wrong *before* the prompt, (3) be correct *after* the prompt, (4) be wrong *after* the prompt, or (5) not respond. If the child is wrong before the prompt on 25% or more for two or more days, then teach the child to wait for the prompt (Wolery et al., 1992). Waiting is often taught in one-to-one sessions. The child is shown abstract symbols that have no names. The teacher shows a symbol and asks the child, "What's this?" and waits about half a second, tells the child a name, and then reinforces the child for imitating the name. Gradually the length of time the teacher waits is increased. The only way the child can be correct is to wait for the teacher to tell what the correct answer is, because none of the symbols have names. Sometimes the teacher will gently hold his or her hand up to the child's mouth to add an additional cue to wait. You could also use a shorter response interval, or switch to progressive time delay if you are using constant time delay. If the child is wrong after the prompt on 25% or more trials for two or more days, use a more controlling prompt. If the child does not respond to 25% or more trials for two or more days, then use a better reinforcer. If the child is correct after the prompt on 90% or more trials for three consecutive days, begin to provide a more desirable reinforcer for correct responses *before* the prompt than for those after the prompt.

Step 10: Implement the Plan and Monitor its Use and Effects

You must plan carefully to successfully embed and distribute time delay. Many distractions in the classroom can occur that might prevent you from embedding and distributing the teaching and using time delay correctly. Correct use, however, is critical. When the prompt is not given as it should be (i.e., when the child waits for help after the task cue), learning will be slow or will not occur (Holcombe, Wolery, & Snyder, 1994). Review the steps frequently (see Table 1) to be sure you are implementing them correctly. Watch what the child does after an embedded trial to ensure that the teaching is not interfering with participation in the activity. Finally, keep track of how many trials are provided each day to be sure enough teaching is occurring.

Summary

Time delay methods give children help on new behaviors and then remove that help so the children can perform the skills independently. Time delay has been studied extensively in direct teaching situations, and some research has been done on time delay embedded and distributed within and across activities and routines. Careful planning using the steps described in this article will help you use time delay within the regular activities of inclusive classrooms. When time delay is used correctly and with enough trials, children often learn new skills quickly.

Notes

You can reach Mark Wolery by e-mail at mark.wolery@vanderbilt.edu

This manuscript was supported by the U.S. Department of Education, Office of Special Education and Rehabilitative Services, Directed Research Projects (Grant No. H324D000039 to Vanderbilt University). However, the opinions expressed do not necessarily reflect the policy of the U.S. Department of Education, and no official endorsement should be inferred.

References

Ault, M. J., Gast, D. L., & Wolery, M. (1988). Comparison of progressive and constant time delay procedures in teaching community sign word reading. *American Journal of Mental Retardation, 93*(1), 44-56.

Bricker, D., Pretti-Frontczak, K., & McComas, N. (1998). *An activity-based approach to early intervention* (2nd ed.). Baltimore: Paul H. Brookes.

Caldwell, N. K., Wolery, M., Werts, M. G., & Caldwell, Y. (1996). Embedding instructive feedback into teacher-student interactions during independent seatwork. *Journal of Behavior Education, 6*(2), 459-480.

Chiara, L., Schuster, J. W., Bell, J., & Wolery, M. (1995). Small group massed-trial and individually distributed-trial instruction with preschoolers. *Journal of Early Intervention, 19*(3), 203-217.

Doyle, P. M., Wolery, M., Ault, M. J., Gast, D. L., & Wiley, K. (1989). Establishing conditional discriminations: Concurrent versus isolation-intermix instruction. *Research in Developmental Disabilities, 10*(4), 349-362.

Dunlap, G. (1984). The influence of task variation and maintenance tasks on the learning and affect of autistic children. *Journal of Experimental Child Psychology, 37*(1), 41-64.

Holcombe, A., Wolery, M., & Snyder, E. (1994). Effects of two levels of procedural fidelity with constant time delay on children's learning. *Journal of Behavioral Education, 4*(1), 49-73.

Mulligan, M., Guess, D., Holvoet, J., & Brown, F. (1980). The individualized curriculum sequencing model (1): Implications from research on massed-, distributed-, or spaced-trial training. *Journal of the Association for the Severely Handicapped, 5*(4), 325-336.

Sandall, S., McLean, M. E., & Smith, B. J. (2000). *DEC recommended practices in early intervention/early childhood special education.* Longmont, CO: Sopris West.

Schwartz, I. S., Anderson, S. R., & Halle, J. W. (1989). Training teachers to use naturalistic time delay: Effects on teacher behavior and on the language use of students. *Journal of the Association for Persons With Severe Handicaps, 14*(1), 48-57.

Venn, M. L., Wolery, M., Werts, M. G., Morris, A., DeCesare, L. D., & Cuffs, M. S. (1993). Embedding instruction in art activities to teach preschoolers with disabilities to imitate their peers. *Early Childhood Research Quarterly, 8*(3), 277-294.

Werts, M. G., Wolery, M., Venn, M. L., Demblowski, D., & Doren, H. (1996). Effects of transition-based teaching with instructive feedback on the acquisition of skills by children with and without disabilities. *Journal of Educational Research, 90*(4), 75-86.

Wolery, M. (1994). Implementing instruction for young children with special needs in early childhood classrooms. In M. Wolery & J. S. Wilbers (Eds.), *Including children with special needs in early childhood programs* (pp. 151-166). Washington, DC: National Association for the Education of Young Children (NAEYC).

Wolery, M. (2000). Recommended practices in child-focused interventions. In S. Sandall, M. E. McLean, & B. J. Smith (Eds.), *DEC recommended practices in early intervention/early childhood special education* (pp. 29-37). Longmont, CO: Sopris West.

Wolery, M., Anthony, L., & Heckathorn, J. (1998). Transition-based teaching: Effects on transitions, teachers' behavior, and children's learning. *Journal of Early Intervention, 21*(2), 117-131.

Wolery, M., Anthony, L., Snyder, E. D., Werts, M. G., & Katzenmeyer, J. (1997). Training elementary teachers to embed instruction during classroom activities. *Education and Treatment of Children, 20*(1), 40-58.

Wolery, M., Ault, M. J., & Doyle, P. M. (1992). *Teaching students with moderate and severe disabilities: Use of response prompting strategies.* White Plains, NY: Longman.

Resources
Within Reason
Teaching Strategies

Here you'll find additional resources to support the recommended practices in child-focused interventions. These resources range in price. Many are within an individual's budget while others may be more suitable for acquisition by a program, agency, or school.

Camille Catlett, M.A., University of North Carolina at Chapel Hill

Books and Media

Cultural Diversity and Social Skills Instruction: Understanding Ethnic and Gender Differences
by Gwendolyn Cartledge & JoAnne Fellows Milburn

Here's a book that offers ideas for teaching social skills from a culturally sensitive perspective. It affirms that the behaviors of culturally and linguistically diverse young children need to be viewed from a cultural perspective and addresses how instruction should affirm and empower children. The authors address differences in social skills according to ethnicity, gender, and other variables. (Champaign, IL: Research Press)

Designing Preschool Interventions: A Practitioner's Guide
by David W. Barnett, Susan H. Bell, & Karen T. Carey

"Practical" and "ecological" are the two words most often used to describe this text. One reviewer said that it " ... captures the essence of what it takes to provide high quality intervention services to preschoolers experiencing developmental delays and disabilities as well as those

who are at risk" (http://www.guilford.com/cartscript.cgi?page=edu/
barnett3.htm&cart_id=208429.9605). Both relevant research and practical examples are cited in chapters that cover topics from the classroom
as ecosystem to designing effective interactions. (New York: Guilford)

Early Childhood Inclusion: Focus on Change
by Michael J. Guralnick, Editor

Several chapters in this recently published book deserve mention. Mary
Beth Bruder's chapter (*Inclusion of Infants and Toddlers: Outcomes and
Ecology*) offers suggestions for adults who, within and across environments, support opportunities, activities, and routines to promote learn-
ing and participation for our youngest children. McWilliam, Wolery, and
Odom (in *Instructional Perspectives in Inclusive Preschool Classrooms*)
explore key considerations for preschoolers, such as individualized
instruction, skills to be taught, and factors influencing implementation.
And Guralnick (*Social Competence With Peers and Early Childhood
Inclusion: Need for Alternative Approaches*) offers new insights for
developing social skills in infants, toddlers, and young children.
(Baltimore: Paul H. Brookes)

Including Children With Special Needs in Early Childhood Programs
by Mark S. Wolery & Jan S. Wilbers

This book will appeal to teachers and caregivers alike. It provides a
thoughtful synthesis of the research and clear implications and applica-
tions for daily practice. The chapters on designing inclusive environments and implementing instruction for young children with special
needs are particularly useful. (Washington, DC: National Association for
the Education of Young Children [NAEYC])

Talking With Preschoolers: Strategies for Promoting First and Second Language Development
by the Child Development Division, California Department of Education

This videotape is designed to help preschool team members and family
members to develop skills and strategies for meeting the needs of culturally and linguistically diverse children. The tape is organized in short
segments on different aspects of language, listening, and literacy development, suitable for introducing key concepts. A companion print
resource (*Fostering the Development of a First and a Second Language*

in Early Childhood: Resource Guide) offers additional materials for teaching, training, and staff development.

Attn. Jackie Black
California Department of Education
CDE Press
P.O. Box 271
Sacramento, CA 95812-0217
(916) 445-1260
(800) 995-4099
FAX (916) 323-0823
jblack@cde.ca.gov
http://www.cde.ca.gov/cdepress/

Curricula

Play Time, Social Time: Organizing Your Classroom to Build Interaction Skills

by Sam L. Odom, Scott R. McConnell, Michaelene Ostrosky, Carla Peterson, Annette Skellenger, Richard Spicuzza, Lynette K. Chandler, & Mary A. McEvoy

This curriculum guide provides guidelines, activities, and lesson plans to promote social interaction and social competence in preschool children with disabilities or at risk for developmental problems. The program is designed to include peers who are either developing normally or have higher levels of social competence. The curriculum focuses on six social interaction skills: sharing, persistence, requesting to share, play organizing, agreeing, and helping. Highlights include chapters on implementing social skill lessons (with a sample intervention schedule for 100 days), ways to promote generalization, and ways to adapt the curriculum to different situations.

Institute on Community Integration
University of Minnesota
150 Pillsbury Drive SE
109 Pattee Hall
Minneapolis, MN 55455
(612) 624-4512
FAX (612) 624-9344
publications@icimail.coled.umn.edu
http://ici/umn.edu/products/default.html

Skillstreaming in Early Childhood: Teaching Prosocial Skills to the Preschool and Kindergarten Child

by Ellen McGinnis & Arnold P. Goldstein

The *Skillstreaming* approach is designed to help young children develop competence in dealing with interpersonal conflicts, learning to use self-control, and contributing to a positive learning environment. Modeling, role playing, performance feedback, and transfer are featured approaches. The curriculum contains 40 skill lessons and includes six skill groups: beginning social skills, school-related skills, friendship-making skills, dealing with feelings, alternatives to aggression, and dealing with stress. (Champaign, IL: Research Press)

SPIES: Strategies for Preschool Intervention in Everyday Settings
by Sarah Rule & Tim G. Smith

SPIES was developed to introduce adults to intervention strategies that can be used with infant, toddler, and preschool children who have disabilities, special health needs, or are at risk for the development of a disability. Using everyday settings as the context for intervention, these training materials (participant manuals, instructor manuals, videotapes) introduce strategies adults can use in the context of daily routines wherever they happen—in homes, preschools, child care settings, and in the community. The *SPIES* curriculum is divided into six modules: creating teaching opportunities, providing help, incidental teaching, tracking progress, prior to preschool, and planning across the day. An abbreviated version (CD-ROM disc and participant manual for all six modules) and Spanish language captioning are also available.

Attn. Connie Panter
Center for Persons With Disabilities
Utah State University
6800 Old Main Hill
Logan, UT 84322-6800
(435) 797-1993
FAX (435) 797-3944
connie@cpd2.usu.edu
http://www.cpd.usu.edu/SPIES

To order more copies of
Teaching Strategies: What to do to Support Young Children's Development, contact:

Sopris West
(800) 547-6747
4093 Specialty Place
Longmont, CO 80504
www.**sopriswest**.com

y^{Ou}n_g

E x c e p t i o n a l
children